Peter Killingley graduated from Durham University in the UK in 1982. He has been teaching English since 2003 and has taught in Europe, North Africa, the Middle East and Asia. He particularly enjoys teaching exam classes, having first started preparing students for the IELTS exam in 2003. He has a CELTA® and a Trinity Diploma and is currently working for the Australian Centre for Education (ACE) in Phnom Penh, Cambodia.

Mary Kuder graduated from the University of Minnesota in Minneapolis, Minnesota, USA, in 1982. More recently, in May 2015, she received her Master of Arts in English as a Second Language (MA ESL) from Hamline University in St. Paul, Minnesota, USA. She is the editor and researcher of the Glossary of Compensation and Benefits Terms (WorldatWork, 2002), published with the Library of Congress, and the editor of the eBook *100 Points to Consider Before Moving or Retiring in Ecuador* (Crowder, 2013). She has been teaching English since 2013 and has taught in the USA, Ecuador, Cambodia and Mexico. She is currently a professor of English at Centro de Idiomas, Universidad Technológica de la Mixteca in Oaxaca, Mexico.

IELTS TOPIC VOCABULARY: ESSENTIAL VOCABULARY FOR THE SPEAKING AND WRITING EXAMS

Peter Killingley
Mary E. Kuder

AUSTIN MACAULEY PUBLISHERS™

LONDON • CAMBRIDGE • NEW YORK • SHARJAH

A CIP catalogue record for this title is available from the British Library.

ISBN 9781786938671 (Paperback)
ISBN 9781786938688 (Hardback)
ISBN 9781528952118 (ePub e-book)

www.austinmacauley.com

First Published (2020)
Austin Macauley Publishers Ltd
25 Canada Square
Canary Wharf
London
E14 5LQ

Acknowledgements

The authors would like to thank all the students and teachers they have worked with over the years, especially those at ACE Santhor Mok, Phnom Penh, but most especially, Phil Manchester, who reviewed the book prior to publication; students Kim Miratorimoonlight and Hok Vanthanak for their invaluable review, suggestions, comments, questions and feedback; and, indeed, all of the students in their IELTS preparation classes who were given a few sections of the book for homework and who also provided invaluable feedback, comments, review and suggestions.

TABLE OF CONTENTS

Disclaimer

The information contained in this book, and other books in this series by these authors, is for information only and is designed to be used by students who are studying for the IELTS exam. Tips, methods, strategies and suggested responses are only recommendations by the author. Additionally, the information contained in this book is presented "as is". It is provided without any representation or endorsement, and without warranty of any kind, express or implied, including but not limited to the implied warranties of satisfactory quality, fitness of use for a particular purpose, non-infringement, compatibility, security, and accuracy. The author has made reasonable efforts to provide current, accurate and complete information to his readers. The author will not be held liable for any unintentional errors, omissions, or inaccuracies in advice, or any decision made or action taken or not taken in reliance upon the advice and information in this book. If legal advice or other expert assistance is required, the services of a competent professional should be sought.

The material found in this book may include information by third parties. Third party materials may contain opinions as expressed by their owners or the work-product of persons unknown to this author. As such, the author does not assume any responsibility or liability for any third party material or opinions or the work-product of persons unknown to this author. Having such third party material in this book does not constitute the author's guarantee of any information, instruction, or opinion contained within the third-party material.

Permission to reproduce items where third-party owned material protected by copyright is included has been sought and cleared where possible. Every reasonable effort has been made to trace copyright holders, but if any items requiring clearance have been unwittingly included, the author will be pleased to make amends at the earliest possible opportunity.

IELTS is a registered trademark of the University of Cambridge ESOL, the British Council and IDP Education Australia.

This book contains material protected under International and Federal Copyright Laws and Treaties. By payment of the required fees, you have been granted the non-exclusive, non-transferrable right to access and read the text of this eBook on screen. No part of this text may be reproduced, transmitted, downloaded, decompiled, reverse engineered, or stored in or introduced into any informational storage and retrieval system, in any form or by any means, whether electronic or mechanical, now known or hereinafter invented, without the prior written consent of the author.

Cover Design by Sandy MacGowan

Introduction
The Rationale Behind This Book

IELTS Scholar: IELTS Topic Vocabulary evolved from worksheets developed for students who are preparing for the IELTS exam at the Australian Centre for Education, Cambodia, and was written to help you improve your vocabulary when working towards the International English Language Testing System (IELTS) examination. The IELTS English examination is administered by the University of Cambridge Local Examinations Syndicate, The British Council and IDP Education Australia. The aim was to impart a large amount of vocabulary in a short space of time. Although there are some good vocabulary books on the market, none could be found to meet this need.

This book contains topic-specific vocabulary for the IELTS exam and is divided into 20 separate topics including Globalisation, Money and Finance, Food, Sport and Leisure, Politics, Travel and Transport, Media, Architecture, Town and Country, Family, Social Issues, Music and the Arts, Advertising, Education, Crime, Environment, Geography, Health and Medicine, Science and Technology, and Work. There are also sections on collocations, idioms and useful words that can be used when writing essays. It is important that you use collocations when writing and idiomatic language in the speaking exam. The format is clear and easy to use, and includes full instructions and an answer key.

The vocabulary will help you with all parts of the exam, but particularly with the speaking and writing sections. It is, therefore, intended that the vocabulary becomes active and that you actually use it in the exam. This is important, as a good range of vocabulary is one of the criteria used to assess both the speaking and writing components of the exam. Research suggests that in order for a word to become active, it must be encountered at least seven times. The same words have, therefore, been included in a number of exercises so that the student comes across them on a number of occasions. It is important, however, that you work independently to learn the vocabulary.

Learning Vocabulary

It is important that you keep a vocabulary book and record words in it (including the words in this book) and extra information related to them. This information should include such things as the phonemic spelling of the word, word stress, and the part of speech, as well as the definition of the word and an example sentence showing how the word is used. In order to do this, it is necessary to have a good monolingual advanced learner's dictionary.

It is also important to develop techniques, such as mnemonics, to help learn and remember the words. One good system is to have word cards; you write the words in English on one side of the card and in your own language on the other side. You should then look at the word in English and check that you know what it is in your own language, and vice versa. If there are two of you, one could explain or give a definition of the word, and the other could say what the word is. You could also test each other on the spelling of the words. Finally, it would be a good idea to spend a couple of minutes memorising the words in each section when you have completed the activities. Then, without looking at them, write down all the words you can remember.

Finally, it is important that you make the vocabulary active. Try to use the words when you are practising the speaking component of the exam and when practising writing essays. In the exam itself, for part two of the speaking exam, when you are making notes for your short speech, you should write down some of the words you have learned, which you should try to use when you are speaking. Remember, it is important to use a wide range of vocabulary in the exam.

The Organisation of This Book and How to Use It

The main part of this book consists of 20 sections of 24 words, each relating to a topic relevant to the IELTS exam. This means that there are 480 words in total. The words are split into groups of four, and you have to match the words to their corresponding definitions. Immediately after each matching task, there are 12 gapped sentences. You should complete the sentences with a word from the previous exercise. To do this, it may be necessary to change the form of the word in some way. After each unit, there is a word search containing 10 words from that unit. After every four units, there is a 'Stop and Check' section in which you have to match words from the previous units with the phrases highlighted in bold in each of four short paragraphs. Finally, at the end of the book there is a 'Test your Knowledge' section, in which you have to complete the definitions by completing the gaps in the words. This section contains all the words from all twenty units of the book. After this, you can find the units on collocations, idioms and useful words for the essays. At the very end of the book, there is an index for each topic and a complete index containing all the words. The words in both are listed alphabetically.

Abbreviations Used in This Book

As the IELTS exam was originally developed for students who wished to study in Britain or Australia, we have attempted to use British spelling and vocabulary wherever possible. It should be noted, however, that the IELTS exam is now widely accepted by many universities in the U.S.A. We have indicated words that are specifically used in the U.K. with the abbreviation BE and those that are used specifically in the U.S. with AE. Other abbreviations used in this book are (n.) for noun, (v.) for verb, and (adj.) for adjective. These are used where a word is also commonly used as another part of speech.

Unit 1: Globalisation

Economics and Business

Match the words in column A with the definitions in column B.

A	B
(1) stocks and shares c	(a) a place where stocks and shares are bought and sold
(2) consumption b	(b) the act of buying and then using a product or service
(3) stock market a	(c) documents that show that you own part of a company
(4) manufacturing d	(d) the act of making/producing something using machinery

A	B
(1) trade barrier c	(a) a situation where prices increase
(2) immigrate d	(b) possessing abundant wealth
(3) affluence b	(c) regulations that prevent trade between countries
(4) inflation a	(d) to arrive in a new country to start a new life

A	B
(1) prosperity d	(a) a government tax on imports
(2) tariff a	(b) when a company gets another company to do work for it which it could have done itself, often in a foreign country
(3) accounting c	(c) the recording and managing of a company's finances
(4) outsource b	(d) a situation where people are making a lot of money and living a good life

A	B
(1) economic growth _d_	(a) to buy goods from another country
(2) emigration _c_	(b) to sell goods made in your country to another country
(3) export (v.) _b_	(c) a situation where people leave their country to live abroad
(4) import (v.) _a_	(d) a situation where the economy is getting bigger

A	B
(1) the Balance of Trade _c_	(a) a situation where the economy is stagnant or performing badly
(2) recession _a_	(b) a very powerful country with a very strong military and economy, such as the USA or China, which can influence world events
(3) superpower _b_	(c) the difference in value between imports and exports in a particular country
(4) multinational corporation _d_	(d) a company operating in at least one other country outside of its home country

A	B
(1) franchise _b_	(a) how comfortable and wealthy people are in a particular country or area and the value of their possessions
(2) the standard of living _a_	(b) the right to sell a company's goods and/or services in a particular area
(3) taxation _c_	(c) the system of taking money from people by governments to pay for public services like schools, roads, and hospitals and other expenditure
(4) marketing _d_	(d) the action a company takes to try to promote/sell its products and services

Complete the sentences below with a word from this unit. You may have to change the form of the word so that it fits into the sentence grammatically.

1. China has emerged as a major _____ in the world. It has a strong economy and a powerful military.
2. A large number of fast food outlets are _____. They have permission to sell a company's food in a particular place.
3. _____ can be a problem for some countries as often it is the best-educated people who leave to start a new life in a new country. When this happens, it is often referred to as a "brain drain".
4. Apple is a _____ _____. Although it is an American company, a large number of their phones are made in China.
5. A lot of people invest in _____ _____ _____ even though it can be quite risky, as their value can go down as well as up.
6. Thailand _____ a large amount of rice to other countries.
7. The _____ _____ _____ is higher in developed countries than in developing countries. People in developed countries are able to buy more goods and have a more comfortable life.
8. Another word for a _____ is a slump or economic downturn.
9. Some companies in the West _____ some of their work to countries in Asia where labour costs are lower.
10. The _____ of chicken decreases when there is an outbreak of bird flu, as people are afraid to eat it.
11. China experienced sustained _____ _____ during the first decade of the 21st century. As a result, large numbers of people became more affluent.
12. The U.K. _____ rice from Asia as it is not grown in the U.K.

What can you remember?

Now, try to memorise the 24 words in this unit in two minutes. Then, without looking, write down all the words that you can remember.

Globalisation Vocabulary Word Search

Find the words listed below the word search. They may be vertical, horizontal, diagonal, forwards or backwards. Have fun!

E	C	N	E	U	L	F	F	A	L	D	K	G
S	T	E	K	R	A	M	K	C	O	T	S	T
O	K	M	C	U	N	G	S	K	V	E	I	U
G	N	I	T	E	K	R	A	M	O	U	K	I
Y	T	I	R	E	P	S	O	R	P	P	L	I
M	A	N	U	F	A	C	T	U	R	I	N	G
S	A	C	W	K	H	M	L	I	L	A	Y	N
R	E	I	R	R	A	B	E	D	A	R	T	Q
S	M	F	L	T	A	X	A	T	I	O	N	T
C	G	N	I	T	N	U	O	C	C	A	Q	S
O	Z	K	M	F	F	I	R	A	T	P	C	A
X	I	Z	F	D	D	N	H	H	C	T	K	G
F	Q	N	O	I	T	A	L	F	N	I	F	N

accounting ✓	prosperity ✓
affluence ✓	stock market ✓
inflation ✓	tariff ✓
manufacturing ✓	taxation ✓
marketing ✓	trade barrier ✓

17

Unit 2: Money and Finance

Match the words in column A with the definitions in column B.

A	B
(1) currency *d*	(a) the extra money you get over time when you save money, or the extra money you have to pay when you borrow money
(2) exchange rate *c*	(b) a bank card you can use to borrow money, which you then have to repay at a later date
(3) interest *a*	(c) the amount of money you get if you change one unit of one country's currency into the currency of another country
(4) credit card *b*	(d) the type of money used in a particular country

A	B
(1) the cost of living *c*	(a) the money you have to pay for some kind of service
(2) fee *a*	(b) money in the form of notes and coins as opposed to credit or debit cards and such like
(3) cash *b*	(c) the average cost of everyday items in a particular area or country
(4) invest *d*	(d) to buy something in the hope that it will increase in value in the future, when you can sell it and make a profit, or to put money into a business venture

A	B
(1) bank loan *d*	(a) when a company or individual has failed financially and is unable to pay others the money they owe
(2) bankrupt *a*	(b) the money you get (from a fund you and/or your employer have previously paid into while you were working) when you are old and no longer working
(3) pension *b*	(c) when you buy something and pay for it at a later date
(4) on credit *c*	(d) money you borrow from a bank and repay with interest at a later date

A	B
(1) mortgage *b*	(a) a time when it is difficult to borrow money from banks or other places that lend money
(2) overdraft *c*	(b) the money you borrow to buy a house which you owe the bank and which must be repaid to them with interest over a certain amount of time
(3) rebate *d*	(c) the money you owe the bank because you have taken more money out of your account than you had in it
(4) credit crunch *a*	(d) the money you get back when you have paid too much for something, such as taxes

A	B
(1) deposit (n.) *d*	(a) the money you have to pay to the government on your earnings
(2) expenditure *b*	(b) the money you spend
(3) income tax *a*	(c) the illegal economy
(4) black market (n.) *c*	(d) the money you pay to secure the purchase of something before you pay the full amount at a later date

A	B
(1) worthless *c*	(a) wealthy, affluent
(2) priceless *d*	(b) a bank card you can use to take money out of your bank account
(3) well off *a*	(c) not worth anything or not useful
(4) debit card *b*	(d) very valuable or precious

Complete the sentences below with a word from this unit. You may have to change the form of the word so that it fits into the sentence grammatically.

1. The _____ _____ _____ in the U.S.A. is much higher than in China, as things in the U.S. are much more expensive.
2. Some people don't like paying _____ _____. They think they should keep all the money they earn and shouldn't have to give any of it to the government.
3. At the current _____ _____ the dollar is strong compared to other currencies. It means imports for the U.S. are cheaper and exports are more expensive.
4. If you want to buy a house, you need to take out a _____, which you then repay to the lender over a long period of time.
5. After buying the diamonds, the customer found out that they were counterfeit and completely _____.
6. If you pay too much tax, you should get a tax _____. The tax authorities will give you back the amount that you have overpaid.
7. Lawyers' _____ are so high that only the wealthy can afford them.
8. It is a good idea to take out a _____ when you are young so you can live comfortably when you retire.
9. It is illegal to buy something on the _____ _____, which is completely unregulated.
10. You can use a _____ _____ to take money out of your bank account.
11. You can use a _____ _____ to borrow money in the short term. In the U.K. and the U.S., if you repay the money fairly quickly, you don't have to pay interest on it.
12. Some famous works of art are _____. Only the very wealthy can afford to buy them.

What can you remember?

Now, try to memorise the 24 words in this unit in two minutes. Then, without looking, write down all the words that you can remember.

Money and Finance Vocabulary Word Search

Find the words listed below the word search. They may be vertical, horizontal, diagonal, forwards or backwards. Have fun!

Y	F	E	X	O	S	J	H	V	Q	I	C	C
M	C	M	T	V	E	O	C	Q	N	N	A	O
R	T	B	X	E	X	C	N	Z	H	T	S	F
L	I	A	R	R	P	W	U	J	S	E	H	G
Y	S	N	I	D	E	E	R	I	O	R	Y	U
X	O	K	N	R	N	L	C	L	Y	E	W	L
T	P	R	V	A	D	L	T	Z	N	S	B	B
Z	E	U	E	F	I	O	I	L	U	T	W	S
L	D	P	S	T	T	F	D	Z	W	A	G	A
Q	M	T	T	E	U	F	E	U	R	N	P	L
D	W	L	C	Q	R	J	R	Q	M	B	X	C
F	T	W	V	T	E	K	C	D	H	K	R	R
Y	Q	U	K	C	U	R	R	E	N	C	Y	T

bankrupt	expenditure
cash	interest
credit crunch	invest
currency	overdraft
deposit	well off

21

Unit 3: Food

Match the words in column A with the definitions in column B.

A	B
(1) beverage *d*	(a) a waxy substance in your blood, too much of which can be harmful
(2) overweight *c*	(b) food that has been made different in some way by changing its DNA
(3) cholesterol *a*	(c) fat; obese
(4) genetically modified *b*	(d) a drink

A	B
(1) vitamins *a*	(a) essential organic compounds that the body needs in small amounts to stay healthy
(2) balanced diet *b*	(b) eating the right amount of different types of food to stay healthy
(3) organic *c*	(c) grown naturally, without the use of artificial fertilizers, pesticides, or chemicals
(4) vegetarian (n.) *d*	(d) a person who does not eat meat or fish

A	B
(1) malnourished *c*	(a) important substances necessary for good health
(2) nutrients *a*	(b) a greasy solid found in meat and plants that provides energy in your diet; eating too much of it can be harmful
(3) snack (n.) *d*	(c) underfed; not having enough to eat or enough of the right kinds of food which provide the necessary nutrients
(4) fat (n.) *b*	(d) a small amount of food eaten between regular meals

A	B
(1) canteen (BE)/ refectory (BE) *d*	(a) a serving; the amount of a specific food deemed suitable for one person
(2) obesity *c*	(b) the amount of energy that food will produce; if you eat too many you will get fat
(3) calorie *b*	(c) a situation where people are extremely fat/ overweight
(4) portion *a*	(d) an eating place at work or university/college

A	B
(1) protein *c*	(a) food that you can get very quickly, such as hamburgers and pizza
(2) carbohydrate *b*	(b) a naturally occurring substance found in food that gives you energy
(3) confectionery *d*	(c) a substance found in meat, fish, eggs, and beans which is an essential part of one's diet
(4) fast food *c*	(d) sweets and chocolate

A	B
(1) allergy *a*	(a) an intolerance to a particular type of food which causes an adverse reaction when eaten
(2) have a healthy appetite *b*	(b) to have the desire to eat a good amount of food
(3) food poisoning *c*	(c) when you become sick as a direct result of eating contaminated food
(4) minerals *d*	(d) naturally occurring, important substances in food, such as calcium and iron

Complete the sentences below with a word from this unit. You may have to change the form of the word so that it fits into the sentence grammatically.

1. She became a _____ when she was very young; she stopped eating meat because she was worried about the welfare of animals.
2. _____ is a big problem in most countries and is caused by a poor diet, overeating and a lack of exercise.
3. People should eat a _____ _____, including a lot of fruit and vegetables and not too much meat.
4. Poor food hygiene can cause _____ _____, the symptoms of which include diarrhoea and vomiting.
5. It is not a good idea to eat too many _____ between meals.
6. During a famine, many people are _____, as there is not enough food to go around.
7. It is not a good idea to eat too much _____ _____, such as burgers and pizza.
8. It is recommended that people eat at least five _____ of fruit and vegetables every day.
9. The _____ at work has affordable, subsidised food.
10. If you are _____, you should go on a diet, as weighing too much is very bad for your long-term health.
11. Citrus fruit, such as oranges and lemons, is a good source of _____ C and other essential nutrients.

What can you remember?

Now, try to memorise the 24 words in this unit in two minutes. Then, without looking, write down all the words that you can remember.

Food Vocabulary Word Search

Find the words listed below the word search. They may be vertical, horizontal, diagonal, forwards or backwards. Have fun!

E	J	Y	G	R	E	L	L	A	P	L	W	Y
G	T	K	Z	J	N	I	E	T	O	R	P	L
J	U	Q	Q	S	F	O	A	R	G	R	V	U
W	O	B	R	O	R	R	E	V	Z	P	N	H
K	O	X	G	G	O	T	E	Y	M	X	S	I
O	V	Q	A	E	S	M	Q	G	L	L	H	Q
C	O	N	F	E	C	T	I	O	N	E	R	Y
Q	I	D	L	B	E	V	E	R	A	G	E	S
C	I	O	Z	G	V	D	H	A	A	X	R	U
V	H	S	Z	Y	C	V	O	A	F	A	S	S
C	W	R	S	U	O	I	T	I	R	T	U	N
S	L	A	R	E	N	I	M	J	W	A	Y	S
T	O	W	L	R	R	T	G	J	V	Z	A	T

allergy	fast food
beverage	minerals
calorie	nutritious
cholesterol	organic
confectionery	protein

Unit 4: Sport and Leisure

Match the words in column A with the definitions in column B.

A	B
(1) lifestyle c	(a) what you do in your free time that involves other people
(2) recreational d	(b) a lazy person who sits in front of the TV all day and gets very little exercise
(3) social life a	(c) the sort of life you have and the things you do
(4) couch potato b	(d) related to leisure/your free time

A	B
(1) bungee jumping b	(a) jumping off mountains and floating around while attached to a parachute
(2) scuba diving d	(b) an activity where you jump from a very high structure, like a bridge, while attached to a stretchable rubber cord and then bounce up and down
(3) paragliding a	(c) walking long distances in the countryside or mountains over a period of days or even weeks
(4) trekking c	(d) swimming underwater using special breathing apparatus

A	B
(1) tenpin bowling d	(a) the people who go to watch an event, especially a sporting event
(2) spectators a	(b) a large building where people go to watch a sporting event
(3) stadium b	(c) a person who watches a game, makes decisions, and penalises players or teams in order to ensure that they follow the rules
(4) referee c	(d) an activity where you roll a hard rubber or plastic ball down a track in order to knock down skittles

A	B
(1) gymnastics _d_	(a) to go to the countryside and eat a pre-packed meal in the open air
(2) running track _c_	(b) a group of people who play a particular sport from whom a team is picked
(3) squad _b_	(c) an artificial surface, usually in the shape of an oval, where athletes can run and compete in sporting events like running races
(4) have a picnic _a_	(d) a sport involving complex body movements and special equipment, such as uneven bars and balance beams

A	B
(1) sedentary _b_	(a) getting the balance right between work and leisure
(2) work-life balance _a_	(b) not active or not involving physical activity
(3) equestrian _d_	(c) a very long-distance running race
(4) marathon _c_	(d) related to riding horses

A	B
(1) martial arts _c_	(a) to do an activity to help you relax/unwind
(2) take a stroll _b_	(b) to go for a leisurely walk
(3) let off steam _a_	(c) various sports which originated in the Far East as forms of self-defence, such as judo
(4) Jacuzzi _d_	(d) a large hot bath with bubbles in it that massages the body

Complete the sentences below with a word from this unit. You may have to change the form of the word so that it fits into the sentence grammatically.

1. Despite the bad weather, we decided to _____ _____ _____ by the river. The food we had packed was delicious!
2. He's a _____ _____. All he does is sit and watch TV all day.
3. At the weekend, I often _____ _____ _____ in my neighbourhood. It is good exercise and not too strenuous.
4. I really enjoy _____ in the mountains. I normally walk for about four or five hours a day.
5. She has a great _____ _____. She often goes to parties and enjoys meeting new people. She has loads of friends and enjoys going out with them.
6. The football club is going to build a new _____. The one they have at the moment is too small, so not enough people can see their games.
7. He has a very _____ lifestyle. He hardly ever takes any exercise and spends most of his day sitting down.
8. I find playing football is a great way to _____ _____ _____. It really helps me to unwind.
9. The _____ cheered when the athlete broke the world record.
10. It's nice to relax in the _____ after going for a swim.
11. The _____ awarded a penalty for a foul by the goalkeeper.
12. Real Madrid have a large _____ of players from which to pick their team.

What can you remember?

Now, try to memorise the 24 words in this unit in two minutes. Then, without looking, write down all the words that you can remember.

28

Sport and Leisure Vocabulary Word Search

Find the words listed below the word search. They may be vertical, horizontal, diagonal, forwards or backwards. Have fun!

X	L	U	S	E	N	L	R	P	G	A	Y	M
N	A	E	C	F	O	K	F	A	E	H	I	E
M	N	L	I	U	H	G	F	R	Q	P	T	G
A	O	Y	T	S	B	A	G	A	U	I	T	E
R	I	T	S	D	F	F	W	G	E	C	W	E
A	T	S	A	A	E	A	M	L	S	J	N	R
T	A	E	N	U	E	F	V	I	T	M	A	E
H	E	F	M	Q	O	W	G	D	R	U	K	F
O	R	I	Y	S	F	X	Z	I	I	I	X	E
N	C	L	G	F	Q	V	T	N	A	D	J	R
C	E	N	M	E	I	Q	O	G	N	A	U	O
S	R	O	T	A	T	C	E	P	S	T	Z	E
D	M	R	T	B	M	R	H	N	S	S	I	O

equestrian	recreational
gymnastics	referee
lifestyle	spectators
marathon	squad
paragliding	stadium

Stop and Check: Units 1–4

Under each paragraph, write the words from the appropriate unit that correspond with the numbered phrases in bold.

Globalisation

Recently, the world has become one big market and many people [1]**have more money to spend** than at any time in history. People are [2]**buying and using more goods and services** than ever before, and [3]**companies are conducting their operations in many countries.** People, too, are [4]**moving abroad to live permanently.** It can be challenging when [5]**people arrive in a new country to live,** as they have to adapt to a completely different culture. Globalisation itself can cause problems as, for example, when the economy of one country is performing badly it can affect the economies of other countries. This can lead to [6]**economic stagnation** globally, and as a result, the ability to [7]**sell goods to other countries,** for example, will fall. The value of [8]**the money that people have invested in the stock market** also falls dramatically at such times. On the other hand, many people think that globalisation fosters world peace: as countries come to cooperate together in trading goods, they come to know and understand each other better, and disputes are more likely to be resolved through negotiations rather than through armed conflict.

1. _____   5. _____
2. _____   6. _____
3. _____   7. _____
4. _____   8. _____

Money and Finance

People have to manage their finances very carefully. If they use [1]**a bank card to borrow money from the bank** or buy things [2]**with the intention of paying for them at a later date,** they could get into debt. This is partly because we have to pay back [3]**extra money in addition to the money we have borrowed.** This could lead to a [4]**situation where people are unable to pay the money back.** We should also [5]**invest in a scheme when we are working so that we have some money to live on when we retire.** This will ensure that we [6]**have plenty of money** when we are no longer able to work. It is important, in general, that [7]**the money we spend on things** never exceeds our income. This is especially important as sometimes [8]**the price of everyday goods and services** can increase at a greater rate than our income or our pension increases, leaving us with insufficient money.

1. _____	5. _____
2. _____	6. _____
3. _____	7. _____
4. _____	8. _____

Food

It is important that we eat a [1]**good range of food types and not too much of one thing.** We should avoid [2]**unhealthy food from take-aways, such as burgers and fries** and eat more fruit and vegetables. Dieticians recommend that we eat five [3]**servings** of fruit and vegetables every day. We also need to eat meat and fish, however, as they contain [4]**essential substances that the body needs.** We should avoid eating too many [5]**sweets and chocolate** as they contain sugar, which is harmful if eaten in large amounts and can result in [6]**a situation where a lot of people are overweight.** Dark chocolate containing a large amount of cocoa, however, is considered to be beneficial, as it can, among other things, lower blood pressure. We should also take care when we cook food, as poor standards of cleanliness in the kitchen can result in people [7]**becoming ill because of the food they have eaten.** Some people have to avoid eating certain types of food because they have an [8]**adverse reaction** to them when they eat them.

1. _____	5. _____
2. _____	6. _____
3. _____	7. _____
4. _____	8. _____

Sport and Leisure

People spend their leisure time in different ways. Some people are very active and enjoy [1]**taking long walks in the countryside or the mountains,** while others have a lifestyle which [2]**involves hardly any physical activity.** For instance, some [3]**people just sit in front of the television all day long.** Some people enjoy activities that involve a certain amount of risk, such as [4]**jumping off bridges while attached to a stretchable rubber cord.** Others, on the other hand, prefer not to take such risks and instead enjoy safer pursuits such as [5]**going to the countryside and eating food in the open air** or [6]**taking a leisurely walk** in the neighbourhood where they live. Yet other people like to watch sports. Some spectator sports, such as football, are extremely popular, and there are huge [7]**complexes where people go to watch the games.** Whatever we do, it is important that we have [8]**a good balance between the amount of time we spend working and the time we spend enjoying ourselves.**

1. _____	5. _____
2. _____	6. _____
3. _____	7. _____
4. _____	8. _____

Unit 5: Politics

Match the words in column A with the definitions in column B.

A	B
(1) patriotic	(a) having a great love of your country
(2) radical	(b) a system of government in which there is only one political party, and citizens have no freedom of speech or democratic rights
(3) totalitarian	(c) strongly believing in capitalism/the free market
(4) right-wing	(d) very different from what most people think

A	B
(1) left-wing	(a) a person who is applying for a political position
(2) candidate	(b) believing in socialism/equality
(3) nationalism	(c) a political perspective or way of seeing the world, such as conservatism or communism
(4) ideology	(d) when the interests of your country are more important than anything else

A	B
(1) anarchism	(a) a department of government that is responsible for one particular area of interest, like education or defence
(2) committee	(b) a form of government in which a king or queen is in charge
(3) monarchy	(c) an official group of people who meet to make decisions about a particular issue
(4) ministry	(d) an ideology which asserts that laws and governments are not important or necessary

A	B
(1) president	(a) the most important minWister in a government
(2) election	(b) a vote by all the registered voters in a country or area on a particular issue
(3) referendum	(c) the head of state in a republic
(4) prime minister	(d) when people vote for the person/party they want to form a government

A	B
(1) democracy	(a) to choose which party you want to form a government
(2) policy	(b) a system where the people have the power to elect a government of their own choosing
(3)political party	(c) a group of people with similar political beliefs who want to form a government
(4) vote	(d) a proposal on a particular issue

A	B
(1) socialist	(a) a person who believes in preserving traditions
(2) conservative	(b) two or more parties working together to govern the country
(3) coup	(c) when a government is overthrown, usually by the army or armed forces, and is replaced by a new government
(4) coalition	(d) a person who believes in equality and the equal distribution of wealth

Complete the sentences below with a word from this unit. You may have to change the form of the word so that it fits into the sentence grammatically.

1. To be a presidential _____ in the USA you need to have a lot of money, as getting elected there requires spending very large sums of money.
2. An _____ is when people vote for the party they want to govern the country.
3. Republicans and Democrats are two of the _____ _____ in the USA.
4. The two parties decided to work together and form a _____ government.
5. Margaret Thatcher was the first woman to be _____ _____ in the UK.
6. Conservatism, liberalism and socialism are all _____, or different ways of seeing the world politically.
7. Some people in England like the idea of having a king or queen as head of state. They believe in the idea of a _____.
8. Most people are _____ to some extent. They always support their country at the World Cup or other important sporting events.
9. Scotland held a _____ in 2015 to see if people still wanted to be a part of the United Kingdom or to become an independent country.
10. He claimed to be a _____, yet he was rich and selfish.
11. The army staged a _____ and installed a new government.
12. The Republicans are considered to be more _____ - _____ than the Democrats, who are considered to be more left wing.

What can you remember?

Now, try to memorise the 24 words in this unit in two minutes. Then, without looking, write down all the words that you can remember.

Politics Vocabulary Word Search

Find the words listed below the word search. They may be vertical, horizontal, diagonal, forwards or backwards. Have fun!

Y	F	C	I	T	O	I	R	T	A	P	X	Y
M	R	A	X	P	R	E	S	I	D	E	N	T
D	P	T	C	X	S	B	B	S	Q	O	C	T
L	E	H	S	C	Y	C	A	T	C	O	O	F
L	V	M	H	I	T	I	L	C	O	J	M	C
R	B	G	O	J	N	C	O	F	A	G	M	E
A	N	A	R	C	H	I	S	M	L	G	I	D
I	U	Q	E	X	R	M	M	T	I	Y	T	P
Q	C	V	T	K	K	A	R	C	T	C	T	L
A	A	O	B	K	H	O	C	J	I	I	E	F
V	Q	T	X	N	J	J	V	Y	O	L	E	S
W	B	E	Y	R	M	I	Y	E	N	O	Q	Y
Y	H	R	A	D	I	C	A	L	K	P	P	I

anarchism	patriotic
coalition	policy
committee	president
democracy	radical
ministry	vote

Unit 6: Travel and Transport

Match the words in column A with the definitions in column B.

A	B
(1) excursion	(a) a change in the route you are taking in order to avoid something or see something of interest
(2) terminal (n.)	(b) a trip to see a specific place or thing, made for pleasure
(3) all-inclusive	(c) a building where trains, aircraft, and buses leave and arrive
(4) detour	(d) when everything (such as food and drinks) is included in the price of the holiday or hotel

A	B
(1) facilities	(a) being tired after a long flight because of the time difference between the country you left and the one you arrived in
(2) jet lag	(b) the amenities a hotel or place has, such as a swimming pool, restaurant, etc.
(3) cab	(c) very expensive, comfortable hotels, apartments, etc.
(4) luxury accommodation	(d) taxi

A	B
1) check-in (v.)	(a) the place at an airport where you have to show your passport to officials before you can leave or enter a country
(2) ecotourism	(b) a boat or ship that goes back and forth between two places, carrying people, cars, or products
(3) immigration	(c) to register at a hotel or airport
(4) ferry	(d) tourism that is friendly to the environment

A	B
(1) hand luggage	(a) a list of the places you will visit on a tour
(2) aviation	(b) the luggage you can carry onto an aircraft yourself
(3) destination	(c) related to aircraft
(4) itinerary	(d) the place you are going to

A	B
(1) journey (n)	(a) a flight travelling a long distance, normally between two or more continents
(2) long-haul	(b) the process of travelling from one place to another
(3) canal	(c) a flight travelling a short or medium distance, normally within a country or continent
(4) short-haul	(d) a man-made river

A	B
(1) budget accommodation	(a) to get onto a ship
(2) trip (n)	(b) to get off a ship
(3) embark	(c) very cheap places to stay
(4) disembark	(d) a journey undertaken, especially one for pleasure

Complete the sentences below with a word from this unit. You may have to change the form of the word so that it fits into the sentence grammatically.

1. A flight from Bangkok to London is considered to be a _____ - _____ flight.
2. Since the road was closed, we had to take a _____, which added 30 minutes to the journey time.
3. The weight allowance for _____ _____, which you carry on to the aircraft, is about seven kilograms on most airlines.
4. The cross-channel _____ makes regular return trips to carry passengers and their cars between England to France. The journey takes about one and a half hours.
5. The Suez _____, which took 10 years to construct, made it much easier to go by ship from Europe to Asia.
6. In London you can get a black _____ if you want to get around the city, although they are much more expensive than taking a bus.
7. The _____ at the hotel were great. They had an infinity pool and a sauna.
8. After a long-haul flight it is common for people to suffer from _____ _____. This is partly due to the time difference between the country they departed from and the country they arrived in.
9. The _____ industry is dominated by the two largest aircraft manufacturers, Boeing and Airbus.
10. When you get to the airport, you need to _____-_____, to confirm that you will be on the flight, although it is possible to do it online.
11. When you arrive at an airport in a foreign country, before you collect your luggage, you have to go through _____ and show your passport to the officials.
12. The hotel is a good example of _____, as it uses locally sourced materials and solar power.

What can you remember?

Now, try to memorise the 24 words in this unit in two minutes. Then, without looking, write down all the words that you can remember.

Travel and Transport Vocabulary Word Search

Find the words listed below the word search. They may be vertical, horizontal, diagonal, forwards or backwards. Have fun!

T	V	C	A	L	Y	D	B	X	S	K	I	P
I	K	M	O	P	R	K	R	A	B	M	E	K
W	I	Y	R	E	R	V	V	F	N	N	R	Y
O	Y	O	C	V	E	J	U	X	O	A	N	E
M	V	R	F	L	F	C	J	X	B	X	L	N
M	P	U	A	G	Q	G	R	M	S	X	D	R
B	V	N	U	R	I	T	E	D	G	F	E	U
S	A	Z	K	Y	E	S	H	K	N	T	P	O
C	D	E	S	T	I	N	A	T	I	O	N	J
A	E	R	D	D	S	E	I	T	R	I	P	N
J	X	X	L	O	Q	G	A	T	I	S	C	J
J	N	V	E	X	C	U	R	S	I	O	N	O
T	E	R	M	I	N	A	L	Y	B	D	T	T

canal	ferry
destination	itinerary
disembark	journey
embark	terminal
excursion	trip

Unit 7: Media

Match the words in column A with the definitions in column B.

A	B
(1) proprietor	(a) the owner of a business
(2) well-informed	(b) the main heading at the top of an article or page of a newspaper
(3) headline	(c) to transmit a programme on radio or television
(4) broadcast (v.)	(d) knowing a lot about something

A	B
(1) satellite	(a) a person or company that prepares a book, magazine, newspaper, or electronic information so that it is ready to be sold
(2) publisher	(b) when the government places restrictions on what people can say
(3) journalism	(c) the process of writing factual information for publication in a newspaper or on the internet or to be broadcast on television or the radio
(4) censorship	(d) an object that orbits the earth and transmits or collects information

A	B
(1) horoscope	(a) the person who hosts/fronts a programme
(2) episode	(b) one part of a series of programmes
(3) presenter	(c) an arrangement whereby you pay money in advance to read or watch something over a period of time, such as a particular magazine or satellite channel
(4) subscription	(d) something that claims to predict your future based on your date of birth and the movement of the stars and planets

A	B
(1) tabloid	(a) when you see someone, such as actors, musicians, or athletes, performing in person as something is happening (not pre-recorded)
(2) journal	(b) a small, low-quality newspaper
(3) live (event)	(c) a specialist magazine relating to a particular subject
(4) paparazzi	(d) photographers who take photos of famous people

A	B
(1) free press	(a) when you pay to watch a specific event, such as a football match, on television or the internet
(2) pay-per-view	(b) the person who decides what a film, book, or newspaper article should include and will eventually look like
(3) editor	(c) a person who collects and/or reports the news
(4) reporter	(d) when newspapers and television channels can say whatever they like without censorship

A	B
(1) documentary	(a) what is being reported in the news that is happening at the present time
(2) soap opera	(b) a collective word for newspapers, magazines, and journalists
(3) current affairs	(c) a television drama series based on the lives of ordinary, but fictional, people
(4) the press	(d) a factual film about a particular topic

Complete the sentences below with a word from this unit. You may have to change the form of the word so that it fits into the sentence grammatically.

1. The _____ make life difficult for famous people as they are always photographing them and invading their privacy.
2. I couldn't see the football match _____ as I was working. I had to watch a recording when I got home.
3. I always read a newspaper because I want to be _____ - _____ about world events.
4. The _____ on the television about marine life in the Arctic Ocean was fascinating.
5. A large number of people have either cable or _____ television. As a result, they have access to a large number of channels.
6. The _____ of a newspaper usually has the final say about what is included in the paper and its layout.
7. I like watching _____ _____ programmes because I want to know what is happening in the world.
8. In some countries, because of _____, some journalists cannot write what they want to. If they do, they will get into trouble with the government.
9. If we don't have a _____ _____, people won't know what's really happening in the world.
10. Some people like reading their _____ because they think it will tell them what will happen to them in the future.
11. The _____ of a newspaper can put pressure on the editor to change the content of a newspaper. As the owner, they feel that they have the right to do this.
12. According to the _____ on the front page of the newspaper, ten people died in the fire.

What can you remember?

Now, try to memorise the 24 words in this unit in two minutes. Then, without looking, write down all the words that you can remember. Media Vocabulary Word Search

Find the words listed below the word search. They may be vertical, horizontal, diagonal, forwards or backwards. Have fun!

P	S	X	S	N	J	N	L	U	N	F	B	Y
R	X	U	D	O	J	L	V	E	H	B	Q	C
E	R	F	B	B	A	O	A	T	L	Z	V	P
S	E	R	G	S	I	P	A	N	G	C	B	H
E	T	M	H	U	C	B	O	L	R	Q	P	B
N	R	M	V	Q	L	R	Z	P	W	U	S	P
T	O	J	X	O	W	I	I	I	E	B	O	P
E	P	V	I	T	Z	B	K	P	Z	R	B	J
R	E	D	O	S	I	P	E	O	T	W	A	O
B	R	O	A	D	C	A	S	T	Q	I	F	O
N	P	R	O	P	R	I	E	T	O	R	O	D
G	Y	T	M	K	G	P	Z	F	C	V	R	N
J	O	U	R	N	A	L	I	S	M	Y	Z	D

broadcast	proprietor
episode	reporter
journal	soap opera
journalism	subscription
presenter	tabloid

Unit 8: Architecture

Match the words in column A with the definitions in column B.

A	B
(1) demolish	(a) a hard material used in constructing buildings
(2) well-designed	(b) to completely destroy something such as a building
(3) bedsit/studio apartment	(c) designed to serve its purpose well or to be attractive
(4) concrete	(d) an apartment consisting of just one room containing a bed and a living area

A	B
(1) derelict	(a) a high, multi-storied building
(2) construction	(b) very modern, like something might look in the future
(3) high-rise	(c) used to refer to a building in very bad condition; no longer inhabited
(4) futuristic	(d) the process of building something, like a work or living structure, a road or a bridge

A	B
(1) detached house	(a) a platform on the outside of a room on an upper floor of a building that has a low wall or rail around it
(2) balcony	(b) the way a building is constructed using different parts
(3) eyesore	(c) a very ugly building
(4) structure (n.)	(d) a house that is not attached to another house

A	B
(1) insulation	(a) a poor area containing very poor-quality housing
(2) slum	(b) the materials that are used to stop heat or sound from escaping from a building
(3) cottage	(c) a style that is very different from traditional or conventional styles
(4) modernist	(d) a small house in the country

A	B
(1) column	(a) a low building, often with only one or two stories
(2) skyscraper	(b) a pillar used to support the structure of a building
(3) patio	(c) a very high, multi-storied building
(4) low-rise	(d) an flat outside area with a stone or concrete floor adjoining a house where people can sit to relax

A	B
(1) storey (BE)/story (AE)	(a) a level or floor of a building
(2) gated community	(b) a paved area outside a building, similar to a patio
(3) civil engineer	(c) a collection of houses in an area surrounded by a security wall with a guarded entrance
(4) terrace	(d) a person who designs and helps construct roads, bridges, etc.

Complete the sentences below with a word from this unit. You may have to change the form of the word so that it fits into the sentence grammatically.

1. I've always wanted to live in a small _____ in the country.
2. My father is a _____ _____. He helped to build the bridge over the river.
3. When we bought the house it was almost _____, but we have renovated, so that it is now in very good condition.
4. That building is so ugly. It's a real _____.
5. In cold countries, it is important to have _____ in buildings to prevent heat from escaping.
6. They _____ the old houses to make way for a block of flats.
7. That part of the city is a _____. The houses are poorly constructed and have no electricity or running water.
8. It's a twenty-_____ building, so if you want to go to the top, you should take the lift.
9. The _____ of the new supermarket should be completed early next year. The building work is progressing slower than expected.
10. Because of the high crime rate, it is a good idea to live in a _____ _____ as it is more secure.
11. The skyline of New York is dominated by _____, such as the Empire State Building.
12. I live in a _____ _____ surrounded by a large garden. My closest neighbours, who live a short distance away, have a similar house and garden.

What can you remember?

Now, try to memorise the 24 words in this unit in two minutes. Then, without looking, write down all the words that you can remember.

Architecture Vocabulary Word Search

Find the words listed below the word search. They may be vertical, horizontal, diagonal, forwards or backwards. Have fun!

X	S	T	S	I	N	R	E	D	O	M	X	W
U	W	B	H	C	V	H	W	S	F	Z	C	K
Z	V	V	S	O	F	T	E	R	R	A	C	E
X	W	H	I	N	J	Q	S	P	G	U	C	C
J	B	A	L	C	O	N	Y	K	R	I	O	K
D	I	P	O	R	B	P	P	J	T	V	J	Z
K	B	J	M	E	P	E	P	S	A	T	J	L
W	T	I	E	T	H	L	I	O	R	L	X	L
R	V	K	D	E	O	R	B	E	D	S	I	T
I	K	S	E	R	U	T	C	U	R	T	S	A
W	P	P	R	T	D	J	F	N	K	B	B	O
V	W	Z	U	Q	P	A	T	I	O	C	E	B
O	J	F	C	P	C	O	L	U	M	N	C	V

balcony	futuristic
bedsit	modernist
column	patio
concrete	structure
demolish	terrace

47

Stop and Check: Units 5-8

Under each paragraph, write the words from the appropriate unit that correspond with the numbered phrases in bold.

Politics

People differ in their political views. They have different **[1]ways of viewing the world in terms of politics.** In democracies, people are given the opportunity to **[2]choose their governments** at regular intervals. **[3]Groups of people with similar political ideas who want to form a government** compete with other such groups to get the largest number of votes to determine who will govern the country. Some parties have views that are **[4]very different from what is considered to be usual,** while others **[5]believe in keeping things the way they have always been and maintaining traditions.** Between elections, people are often able **[6]to vote on specific issues that concern them.** Not all systems of government are democratic, however, and some countries have **[7]governments which have almost total control over their populations and in which free speech is severely restricted.** Sometimes, such **[8]governments are overthrown, often by the armed forces.** Although many people believe that democracies are the ideal form of government, they do not appear to work in all countries, especially in those countries that do not have a democratic tradition.

1. _____   5. _____
2. _____   6. _____
3. _____   7. _____
4. _____   8. _____

Travel and Transport

Travelling by plane can be quite stressful. When you get to **[1]the airport building where you catch your flight,** you have to **[2]confirm that you will be on the flight.** This can also be done on the internet. You then have to **[3]show your passport to officials who will check it before you can leave the country.** When people arrive at their final stop, they have to go through immigration again before they can pick up their luggage. On short-haul flights, people might only have **[4]luggage that they have taken on the plane with them.** A **[5]long flight between different continents** can be very tiring, and people often arrive suffering from **[6]a condition which makes them very tired, partly due to the time difference between the country they left and the country they arrived in.** This condition can last for a few days. Travellers often get a **[7]taxi** from the airport to a hotel as it saves time, and they can get to their accommodation faster and get much-needed sleep. They can then take advantage of the hotel's **[8]amenities,** such as the swimming pool, gym and restaurant. This can help alleviate many of the stresses associated with travelling.

1. _____ 5. _____
2. _____ 6. _____
3. _____ 7. _____
4. _____ 8. _____

Media

The media is a source of both entertainment and education. In most countries [1]**journalists can write what they want.** In some countries, however, there are [2]**restrictions on what people can say or write about.** The [3]**owner of a newspaper** can also influence what and how news is reported. People read or watch news programmes so that they can keep up to date with [4]**what is happening around the world at the present time.** People read newspapers, watch television and surf the internet not only to be informed, but also to be entertained. They enjoy watching [5]**drama series based on the lives of ordinary people** as well as [6]**factual films that impart knowledge.** It is also possible to watch sporting events [7]**as they are happening,** although sometimes you [8]**have to pay extra money to watch specific matches or events.**

1. _____ 5. _____
2. _____ 6. _____
3. _____ 7. _____
4. _____ 8. _____

Architecture

People live in different types of buildings, ranging from [1]**large houses in their own grounds** to [2]**small apartments containing just one main room.** Some buildings have [3]**only one or two stories,** while others are [4]**many stories high.** New York is famous for having a large number of [5]**very high buildings,** such as the Empire State Building. Some people dream of buying a [6]**small house in the countryside with lots of character,** while others simply want to get out of the [7]**poor, run-down area** in which they are living. Wherever we decide to live, it is important that buildings are [8]**designed in a good way** and are not eyesores. Unfortunately, many cities are losing their character because many modern buildings look the same, and old traditional buildings are being demolished to make way for them.

1. _____ 5. _____
2. _____ 6. _____
3. _____ 7. _____
4. _____ 8. _____

Unit 9: Town and Country

Match the words in column A with the definitions in column B.

A	B
(1) shopping mall	(a) the artificial supply of water for crops
(2) crops	(b) when the number of people living in an area is getting smaller
(3) depopulation	(c) plants that are grown in large quantities to be eaten
(4) irrigation	(d) a very large building containing many shops, restaurants and the like inside.

A	B
(1) rural	(a) an area with a lot of similar houses together
(2) housing estate	(b) relating to the countryside
(3) arable land	(c) a substance, often consisting of chemicals, used on the land in order to increase the amount of crops grown
(4) fertilizer	(d) agricultural land used to grow crops

A	B
(1) megacity	(a) transport that everyone can use, such as buses and trains
(2) public transport	(b) a large, high building containing offices
(3) cosmopolitan	(c) a really big city, usually with a population of more than 10 million people
(4) office block	(d) containing people from lots of different cultures/countries

A	B
(1) traffic congestion	(a) relating to a town/city
(2) infrastructure	(b) when there is too much traffic in one place
(3) urban	(c) the basic facilities in an area, such as bridges, roads, and sewage systems, that are necessary for a society to function properly
(4) beggars	(d) poor people who ask you to give them money

A	B
(1) metropolitan	(a) the area around the edges of a town/city
(2) urban sprawl	(b) an outdoor area, normally containing shops and restaurants, where motorised traffic is banned and people can walk freely
(3) outskirts	(c) relating to a large town/city
(4) pedestrian precinct	(d) when an urban area starts spreading out and taking over areas of countryside

A	B
(1) the rush hour	(a) an area, often residential, away from the centre of a town/city
(2) suburbs	(b) a time when the roads are unusually busy because people are travelling to and from work
(3) inner city	(c) when there are too many people in one place
(4) overcrowding	(d) the central parts of a city

Complete the sentences below with a word from this unit. You may have to change the form of the word so that it fits into the sentence grammatically.

1. London is a very _____ city. People from all over the world live there.
2. As a result of _____ _____, large areas of countryside have been taken over by houses and factories and now have a large number of people living and working there.
3. China has a lot of _____ like Shanghai. In 2010, more than 27 million people were living there.
4. In areas of low rainfall, _____ is necessary in order to water the crops.
5. The countryside has witnessed marked _____ as people have moved to the towns.
6. I live on the _____ of the town. It takes me about one hour to get to the city centre, but there is much less traffic in my area than in the inner city.
7. It is a good idea to avoid travelling during _____ _____ _____ as the roads are very busy with people going to and from work at that time of day.
8. _____ _____ is a major problem in most big cities. It makes getting around difficult and results in an increase in pollution.
9. I would rather live in a _____ area because I like nature.
10. I would rather live in an _____ area because I like the excitement of a big city.
11. If people used _____ _____ more, there would be fewer private vehicles on the road and consequently less traffic congestion.
12. The local authorities are going to build a _____ _____ in the town centre so people can walk around and do their shopping without worrying about the traffic.

What can you remember?

Now, try to memorise the 24 words in this unit in two minutes. Then, without looking, write down all the words that you can remember.

Town and Country Vocabulary Word Search

Find the words listed below the word search. They may be vertical, horizontal, diagonal, forwards or backwards. Have fun!

Q	L	L	A	M	G	N	I	P	P	O	H	S
P	U	Q	U	B	A	I	H	M	P	S	R	E
V	X	L	A	S	P	O	R	C	H	H	R	E
N	A	T	I	L	O	P	O	R	T	E	M	B
X	X	I	L	S	B	R	U	B	H	S	P	Y
R	E	Z	I	L	I	T	R	E	F	W	S	O
H	Z	D	Q	S	U	X	T	Y	B	F	Q	G
O	X	K	C	O	L	B	E	C	I	F	F	O
N	P	T	Z	B	R	W	X	K	W	R	L	V
P	B	E	G	G	A	R	S	L	P	I	H	N
L	Y	P	A	R	A	B	L	E	L	A	N	D
I	K	Y	T	I	C	R	E	N	N	I	Z	K
G	N	I	D	W	O	R	C	R	E	V	O	R

arable land	metropolitan
beggars	office block
crops	overcrowding
fertilizer	shopping mall
inner city	suburbs

Unit 10: Family

Match the words in column A with the definitions in column B.

A	B
(1) stepmother and stepfather	(a) a woman/man whose husband/wife has died
(2) ancestors	(b) people who are related to you and who are still alive
(3) widow/widower	(c) people related to us who lived a long time before we did
(4) relatives	(d) the person your mother or father marries after your biological parents have divorced, or one of them has died

A	B
(1) bachelor	(a) to separate and be no longer legally married to your spouse
(2) divorce (v.)	(b) a man who has never been married
(3) the elderly	(c) a person's child/children or the young of an animal
(4) offspring	(d) a polite word for old people

A	B
(1) engagement	(a) an adult who is responsible for the welfare of a young person who is not their biological child
(2) juvenile (adj.)	(b) a family including relatives who are not closely related, such as uncles and aunts and their children
(3) guardian	(c) an arrangement between two people to marry each other in the future
(4) extended family	(d) relating to young people; immature

A	B
(1) adolescent	(a) a family unit consisting of only parents and their children
(2) maternal	(b) a teenager who is almost an adult
(3) nuclear family	(c) relating to mothers
(4) breadwinner	(d) the person who earns the most money in a family

A	B
(1) paternal	(a) a very old person, especially one suffering from poor health
(2) geriatric (n.)	(b) an old person who is probably no longer working
(3) adoption	(c) relating to fathers
(4) senior citizen	(d) the legal process of becoming the parent of a child who is not your own

A	B
(1) upbringing	(a) when parents decide who their children will marry
(2) genes	(b) brothers or sisters
(3) siblings	(c) how children are raised, educated, and nurtured
(4) arranged marriage	(d) units of heredity which are passed from a parent to their children

Complete the sentences below with a word from this unit. You may have to change the form of the word so that it fits into the sentence grammatically.

1. In some countries _____ _____ are common. People cannot choose who they want to marry.
2. _____ crime is on the increase. The age at which people commit crimes is getting lower and lower and it is now not uncommon for teenagers to receive prison sentences.
3. My _____ came to live in the USA from Italy a few generations ago.
4. I only have one _____, a sister. She is two years older than me.
5. My father is the main _____ in my family. My mother doesn't work.
6. In the U.K. a lot of couples _____ soon after getting married. They often remarry, though.
7. When her parents died at an early age she was put up for _____. She was brought up by her new parents and now regards them as her real parents.
8. He has a large _____ _____, with lots of uncles, aunts and cousins.
9. The _____ need to look after their health as people are likely to have more health problems when they get older.
10. _____ _____ often pay less for public transport because they are no longer earning money.
11. My father remarried, but it is not a problem, as I get on really well with my _____.
12. As a _____ she was responsible for making decisions on her niece's behalf after her niece was orphaned.

What can you remember?

Now, try to memorise the 24 words in this unit in two minutes. Then, without looking, write down all the words that you can remember.

Family Vocabulary Word Search

Find the words listed below the word search. They may be vertical, horizontal, diagonal, forwards or backwards. Have fun!

I	O	V	G	T	M	R	L	M	Y	S	N	Q
M	S	F	G	E	R	I	A	T	R	I	C	F
I	E	O	F	Q	R	H	Y	F	L	E	U	U
A	P	O	B	S	H	S	I	A	Y	L	G	I
D	R	A	K	A	P	W	N	U	Q	Z	N	M
O	E	I	T	I	C	R	F	Y	L	G	I	A
L	L	J	J	E	E	H	I	Z	E	P	G	P
E	A	V	C	T	R	S	E	N	R	V	N	I
S	T	I	A	X	O	N	E	L	G	U	I	G
C	I	M	D	C	E	S	A	I	O	K	R	X
E	V	G	W	V	D	G	X	L	M	R	B	J
N	E	N	G	A	G	E	M	E	N	T	P	M
T	S	K	E	F	F	J	R	I	U	L	U	M

adolescent	maternal
bachelor	offspring
engagement	paternal
genes	relatives
geriatric	upbringing

57

Unit 11: Social Issues

Match the words in column A with the definitions in column B.

A	B
(1) discrimination	(a) organised violence used to frighten people for political purposes
(2) animal rights	(b) treating people differently for unfair reasons, such as the colour of their skin or their gender
(3) refugee	(c) the basic rights that animals should have, such as not being used for medical research or hunted
(4) terrorism	(d) a person who has had to leave their home country for political reasons or to escape from a war or natural disaster

A	B
(1) human rights	(a) permission to live in another country because you are being persecuted in your own country
(2) political asylum	(b) a person who disagrees with the government of their country
(3) dissident (n.)	(c) a person who does not fit into the society they live in because they are different in some way and are often shunned
(4) outcast	(d) the basic rights that all people should have

A	B
(1) ethnic cleansing	(a) a person who lives in an unoccupied building without paying rent
(2) civil rights	(b) to treat someone differently because of their race or skin colour
(3) squatter	(c) killing members of a particular race to eliminate them from a particular area
(4) racism	(d) relating to the rights of people in a society

A	B
(1) genocide	(a) a group in a population who are of a different race or culture than the dominant one
(2) abortion	(b) the killing of a large number of people, often because of their race
(3) homelessness	(c) when a pregnancy is deliberately terminated
(4) ethnic minority	(d) the situation that exists when people don't have a permanent home to live in

A	B
(1) euthanasia	(a) to painlessly end someone's life if they are in pain and are terminally ill
(2) nonconformist	(b) a violent protest about something, resulting in public disorder
(3) extremism	(c) a person who is different and does not follow the normal ways of thinking or behaving
(4) riot (n.)	(d) having ideas that are very radical, such as political or religious ideas

A	B
(1) illegal alien	(a) to bother/annoy someone for sexual reasons
(2) sexual harassment	(b) a person who is living in a country illegally
(3) single-parent family	(c) using illegal drugs for recreational purposes
(4) drug abuse	(d) a family that has only a mother or father

Complete the sentences below with a word from this unit. You may have to change the form of the word so that it fits into the sentence grammatically.

1. He arrived as a _____. He left his country when the war broke out.
2. Because of the high divorce rate, _____ - _____ _____ are now very common. A mother or father often has to bring up their children on their own.
3. _____ _____ is a big problem in inner city areas and, as a result, many people are addicted to heroin and other illegal drugs.
4. She fled her country because of her political views and claimed _____ _____ in Germany.
5. Martin Luther King, Jr. was a key figure in the _____ _____ movement in the U.S.A. He helped to secure equal rights for blacks.
6. _____ is one of the biggest problems today. It is designed to frighten people by using random acts of violence, such as bombings, shootings and public beheadings.
7. The Hmong are an _____ _____ who live in mountainous regions of Vietnam, China, Laos and Thailand. They have their own language and system of writing.
8. The attempts by the police to stop the demonstrations resulted in _____. A lot of property was destroyed, and some people were injured.
9. There are laws against _____ so that people of different sexes and races have equal rights.
10. People who believe in _____ _____ think that we shouldn't experiment on animals.
11. In England, people who still smoke cigarettes are _____. They are shunned by the rest of society.
12. _____ is a controversial issue. Should people have the right to end their own lives if they don't have long to live and are in pain?

What can you remember?

Now, try to memorise the 24 words in this unit in two minutes. Then, without looking, write down all the words that you can remember.

Social Issues Vocabulary Word Search

Find the words listed below the word search. They may be vertical, horizontal, diagonal, forwards or backwards. Have fun!

I	O	C	I	T	U	Y	G	S	G	H	Q	A
M	O	H	L	S	Q	S	I	G	E	J	W	O
E	C	V	L	I	F	T	R	I	N	U	N	U
X	M	Z	E	M	E	H	N	Q	O	G	O	T
T	S	Q	G	R	R	G	O	C	C	O	I	C
R	I	Y	A	O	H	I	S	R	I	P	T	A
E	C	P	L	F	A	R	O	E	D	V	R	S
M	A	L	A	N	A	N	R	T	E	E	O	T
I	R	Y	L	O	J	A	M	T	H	Z	B	B
S	Z	R	I	C	S	M	D	A	Q	B	A	D
M	B	B	E	N	D	U	H	U	S	J	V	Q
K	W	T	N	O	F	H	E	Q	H	F	Z	C
E	I	L	T	N	E	D	I	S	S	I	D	C

abortion	illegal alien
dissident	nonconformist
extremism	outcast
genocide	racism
human rights	squatter

61

Unit 12: Music and Arts

Match the words in column A with the definitions in column B.

A	B
(1) performance	(a) when people stand up and clap after an outstanding performance
(2) standing ovation	(b) a person who knows a lot about, and is very interested in, a particular subject
(3) aficionado	(c) an afternoon performance of a play, film, etc.
(4) matinee	(d) the presentation of a form of entertainment, such as a play

A	B
(1) autobiography	(a) a place where an event or performance takes place
(2) composer	(b) a large group of people who play different classical musical instruments together
(3) venue	(c) a true story someone writes about the things that have happened in their life
(4) orchestra	(d) someone who writes music

A	B
(1) exhibition	(a) a celebration involving a lot of people relating to a specific occasion
(2) poetry	(b) a show or display of art
(3) aesthetic	(c) a type of writing where the sounds of the words are as important as their meanings
(4) festival	(d) related to what is regarded as being beautiful

A	B
(1) non-fiction	(a) factual, true accounts, as opposed to stories written about imaginary events
(2) musical (n.)	(b) imaginary stories written for entertainment purposes
(3) arts and crafts	(c) a film or play containing lots of music, singing, and dancing
(4) fiction	(d) a hobby related to making decorative items for the home

A	B
(1) audience	(a) a play with music, where actors sing instead of speaking
(2) pianist	(b) an outstanding work of art
(3) opera	(c) a person who plays the piano
(4) masterpiece	(d) the people who watch or listen to a performance, such as a play or a concert

A	B
(1) ballet	(a) a painting of a person
(2) art gallery	(b) a type of classical dance involving dancing on the tips of your toes
(3) portrait	(c) a painting of objects that does not include people or a landscape, such as a bowl of fruit
(4) still life	(d) a building where works of art are displayed and viewed

Complete the sentences below with a word from this unit. You may have to change the form of the word so that it fits into the sentence grammatically.

1. The Louvre in Paris is a world famous _____ _____ that houses many famous works of art, such as Leonardo da Vinci's painting the "Mona Lisa".
2. The _____ applauded at the end of the play. They all stood up and clapped because they had enjoyed it so much.
3. I prefer to read _____ - _____. I like to read about real events rather than fictional stories.
4. The Mona Lisa by Leonardo da Vinci is considered to be a _____. It is thought to be one of the best paintings ever painted.
5. Beethoven was a very famous German _____. He wrote many famous musical compositions.
6. I prefer to read _____ because it helps me to relax and escape from reality.
7. He is an _____ of jazz. He loves it and knows everything about it.
8. We couldn't see the play in the evening, so we went to the _____ performance in the afternoon.
9. The artist painted a _____ _____ of a bowl of fruit.
10. The _____ for the concert has yet to be confirmed, but it will probably take place at the football stadium.
11. The play was so good that the audience gave it a _____ _____ at the end. They continued clapping for nearly five minutes.
12. Her _____ contains lots of information about her early life that no one else was aware of.

What can you remember?

Now, try to memorise the 24 words in this unit in two minutes. Then, without looking, write down all the words that you can remember.

Music and the Arts Vocabulary Word Search

Find the words listed below the word search. They may be vertical, horizontal, diagonal, forwards or backwards. Have fun!

W	K	U	G	L	M	E	H	E	O	H	D	L
E	H	B	B	H	P	L	R	X	V	F	F	J
E	D	V	D	K	S	X	U	H	Q	H	M	A
T	C	B	T	S	I	N	A	I	P	R	W	F
I	F	N	V	E	G	M	T	B	C	W	V	E
A	S	E	A	O	S	F	J	I	Y	B	R	S
R	J	L	E	M	L	U	T	T	R	A	N	T
T	T	B	A	A	R	E	A	I	T	L	V	I
R	O	Z	K	C	H	O	K	O	E	L	U	V
O	P	T	C	T	I	W	F	N	O	E	V	A
P	E	N	S	N	M	S	D	R	P	T	T	L
D	R	E	Y	P	B	C	U	G	E	X	T	O
H	A	E	U	O	S	O	S	M	D	P	Z	Y

aesthetic	opera
ballet	performance
exhibition	pianist
festival	poetry
musical	portrait

65

Stop and Check: Units 9–12

Under each paragraph, write the words from the appropriate unit that correspond with the numbered phrases in bold.

Town and Country

Some people prefer to live in ¹**towns and cities,** while others prefer to live in ²**the countryside, away from built-up areas.** Many leave the countryside to live in big cities, resulting in ³**far fewer people living in rural areas.** This can also result in problems in the cities. For example, there are often ⁴**too many people living in a small area** and ⁵**too many vehicles on the road,** resulting in excessive air pollution. Some cities, such as many in China, are ⁶**huge urban areas** with populations that are fairly homogenous, while others, such as London, contain a ⁷**wide mix of people from different countries and cultures.** Some towns are expanding rapidly and ⁸**taking over areas that were once part of the countryside,** resulting, in many such places, in the lack of proper infrastructural facilities.

1. _____   5. _____
2. _____   6. _____
3. _____   7. _____
4. _____   8. _____

Family

People's relationships with their families vary throughout the world. In some societies, for example, the main ¹**family unit consists of parents and their children,** while in others it extends to ²**cousins, uncles, aunts and grandparents.** In some countries, people can choose who they marry, whereas in others, ³**their parents decide who they should marry.** Some children have lots of ⁴**brothers and sisters,** while others have one or none. In most societies, it is normal for people to ⁵**legally end their marriage** when they no longer get on with each other. ⁶**Old people** in Asia are normally looked after by their families, but in the West, they sometimes live in special housing for the elderly and are only visited by ⁷**people who are related to them** infrequently. Old ⁸**people whose spouses have died** can be especially lonely, especially in cultures where they have little contact with their sons and daughters.

1. _____   5. _____
2. _____   6. _____
3. _____   7. _____
4. _____   8. _____

Social Issues

Most societies experience similar problems, such as discrimination. Some people are subjected to [1]**discrimination against them because of the colour of their skin,** while others get into trouble because [2]**theyoppose and criticise their governments,** which are often authoritarian. Yet others are discriminated against because they are [3]**not part of the dominant racial group.** Other [4]**people are shunned by society because they are different in some way.** Indeed, many issues are very controversial and cause widespread disagreement. For example, should people be allowed to make [5]**decisions about whether to end their life if they are terminally ill and in pain?** There is less disagreement, however, about other issues such as [6]**using illegal drugs for recreational purposes** and those who frighten people with [7]**random acts of violence in order to intimidate them for political reasons.** In some cases, [8]**whole communities of people have been killed because of their ethnicity.**

1. _____
2. _____
3. _____
4. _____
5. _____
6. _____
7. _____
8. _____

Music and the Arts

As well as taking part in sports and having hobbies, some people take an interest in reading and the arts. A lot of people enjoy reading [1]**imaginary stories;** others prefer reading [2]**books about real-life events** or [3]**the accounts people have written about their lives.** Some people like visiting [4]**places where paintings are on public display,** where they can see [5]**outstanding works of art,** such as [6]**paintings of people** or [7]**paintings of everyday objects.** There are also [8]**people who are so interested in something that they become experts in it.** Overall, however, having people who enjoy different types of things is what helps to make a society diverse and interesting.

1. _____
2. _____
3. _____
4. _____
5. _____
6. _____
7. _____
8. _____

Unit 13: Advertising

Match the words in column A with the definitions in column B.

A	B
(1) plug (v.)	(a) the type, class, or age of people a company is trying to sell its product to
(2) unique selling point (USP)	(b) a strategy designed to create a demand for a product or service
(3) target audience	(c) something that makes a product different from other products and therefore special
(4) advertising campaign	(d) an informal word used for the act of promoting or advertising a product or service

A	B
(1) cold-calling	(a) very noticeable because it is very prominent or different
(2) personal ads	(b) when a company/organisation gives money to a sports team or event in return for publicity
(3) sponsorship	(c) the practice of selling things by telephone to people who are called at random
(4) eye-catching	(d) advertisements used by people to find new friends, partners, or companions

A	B
(1) jingle	(a) a large roadside sign visible from some distance away that advertises a product or service
(2) logo	(b) an image or design closely associated with a company or product, used for marketing purposes
(3) billboard	(c) when a well-known person promotes a particular product or service
(4) celebrity endorsement	(d) a short tune accompanying an advertisement on television, radio, or the internet

A	B
(1) classified ads	(a) when a company introduces a new product onto the market
(2) product launch	(b) small advertisements placed in a newspaper or online by the general public to sell items that they no longer want or need
(3) brand (n.)	(c) a short, catchy phrase used to sell a product
(4) slogan	(d) a name associated with a specific product or range of products made by a particular company

A	B
(1) hype	(a) an advertisement on radio or television
(2) product placement	(b) a discounted price or special deal used to get people to buy a product or service
(3) commercial (n.)	(c) exaggerated claims about the value of a product or service to make it sound better than it really is
(4) special offer	(d) when a product is seen or used in a television programme or film for advertising purposes

A	B
(1) brand loyalty	(a) a company that specialises in promoting the products and services of others
(2) telesales	(b) advertising delivered in such a way that people are unaware of it as it works on an unconscious level
(3) advertising agency	(c) when customers only purchase a particular brand
(4) subliminal advertising	(d) selling products and services over the phone

Complete the sentences below with a word from this unit. You may have to change the form of the word so that it fits into the sentence grammatically.

1. If you want to find a partner or companion, you can place a _____ _____ on the internet.
2. The company's _____ of the football club means that the club have lots of money to spend on new players. In return, the company is able to promote and advertise its products at the stadium and on the team's shirts.
3. There was a lot of _____surrounding the launch of the new phone, but it turned out to be quite disappointing.
4. The shoes were on _____ _____. They were 50% cheaper than normal.
5. The _____ _____ _____ of this phone is that it has a special device that helps people to locate it when it has been lost. Other phones don't have this feature.
6. As we were driving into the city, we saw a _____ advertising a motel further down the road.
7. The _____ _____ devised a strategy to help the company sell the product.
8. The _____ _____ for the product is young, middle-class, professional adults. These are the people the company thinks are most likely to buy it.
9. _____ _____ are a cheap way of selling things people no longer want or need. You can post them on the internet or place them in a newspaper.
10. A lot of people only buy Apple products rather than the products of their competitors. This is an example of _____ _____.
11. The _____ _____ for the company's newest product involved a series of advertisements on television, radio, and the internet.
12. The _____ on television was very funny and probably resulted in more people buying the product.

What can you remember?

Now, try to memorise the 24 words in this unit in two minutes. Then, without looking, write down all the words that you can remember.

Advertising Vocabulary Word Search

Find the words listed below the word search. They may be vertical, horizontal, diagonal, forwards or backwards. Have fun!

L	X	U	S	E	L	A	S	E	L	E	T	W
O	C	G	P	M	S	S	W	C	S	W	L	W
L	O	Y	W	B	I	L	L	B	O	A	R	D
A	H	A	Y	Z	O	O	M	B	R	A	N	D
J	H	L	B	L	O	G	O	L	G	B	M	H
Y	Z	F	A	M	V	A	E	L	G	N	I	J
T	M	O	I	F	G	N	W	F	P	E	V	J
L	K	K	J	K	W	X	H	E	W	V	T	C
H	C	N	U	A	L	T	C	U	D	O	R	P
F	E	P	I	H	S	R	O	S	N	O	P	S
G	P	G	C	D	B	K	A	E	L	Z	X	R
N	I	C	E	H	W	W	Z	P	X	V	B	Y
C	O	M	M	E	R	C	I	A	L	F	G	M

billboard	logo
brand	product launch
commercial	slogan
hype	sponsorship
jingle	telesales

Unit 14: Education

Match the words in column A with the definitions in column B.

A	B
(1) scholarship	(a) a small study group of students and their tutor at university
(2) seminar (BE)	(b) a formal talk/lesson on a specific subject at university
(3) lecture (n.)	(c) a financial award from an organisation, individual, or government, that helps a student pay for their education
(4) faculty (BE)	(d) a department at a university that is based on an area of study like law or history

A	B
(1) tutorial (BE)	(a) similar to a seminar but with fewer students or just one student
(2) degree	(b) the list of topics that you study on a specific course
(3) syllabus	(c) special technical or scientific words related to a particular area of study/work
(4) terminology	(d) an award/qualification you get when you have successfully completed your studies at university

A	B
(1) undergraduate (n.)	(a) a piece of homework at school or university
(2) postgraduate (n.)	(b) a long, formal piece of written work at university containing original research and normally required in order receive a Master's degree or Ph.D.
(3) dissertation/thesis	(c) a student at university who is studying for their first degree
(4) assignment	(d) a student at university who is studying for a higher degree

A	B
(1) Ph.D.	(a) a higher degree you can study for after a first degree
(2) Master's degree	(b) the highest qualification you can get at university; the abbreviation for 'Doctor of Philosophy'
(3) pupil	(c) a school that provides a free education and is funded by the government
(4) state school	(d) a student at primary or secondary school

A	B
(1) distance learning	(a) the subjects offered by a school or college that can be studied there
(2) graduate (v.)	(b) the ability to read and write
(3) curriculum	(c) to obtain a qualification – especially a degree at university
(4) literacy	(d) learning online/at home without having to attend the university or college which awards the qualification

A	B
(1) illiterate	(a) education from the ages of about five to 11; elementary education
(2) primary education	(b) education from the ages of about 11 to 18
(3) secondary education	(c) higher education – normally at a university
(4) tertiary education	(d) not knowing how to read or write

Complete the sentences below with a word from this unit. You may have to change the form of the word so that it fits into the sentence grammatically.

1. A _____ at secondary school normally has to study at least one foreign language.
2. When I graduate from university, I want to stay on and do a Master's degree and then, after that, a _____.
3. I found the reading very difficult to understand because of all the difficult _____. I was constantly looking up words in my dictionary.
4. I really like the idea of _____ _____. It means you can work where and when you like.
5. When you do a Ph.D., you have to write a _____, which should contain original research and ideas. The Faculty of History at Cambridge University advises students that it should not be more than 80,000 words long.
6. I didn't go to a private school. I went to a _____ _____ because my parents didn't have enough money to pay for private school fees.
7. Being _____ can be a big problem, because if people can't read or write, they won't be able to get a very good job.
8. When I was at university, I never completed my _____ on time. I always handed them in late.
9. _____ _____ is considered by some experts to be more important than secondary education, as the early years of a child's life can have a big influence on their future development.
10. The _____ for the English course includes reading, writing and grammar.
11. The _____ at the school includes most of the science subjects, but not chemistry.
12. Over 200 students attended the _____ on the environment. The lecturer is an expert in her field.

What can you remember?

Now, try to memorise the 24 words in this unit in two minutes. Then, without looking, write down all the words that you can remember.

Education Vocabulary Word Search

Find the words listed below the word search. They may be vertical, horizontal, diagonal, forwards or backwards. Have fun!

Q	E	O	S	Y	C	C	S	U	S	B	O	N
Y	W	T	T	L	I	T	E	R	A	C	Y	G
F	W	K	A	C	T	E	W	C	J	E	R	X
F	L	U	N	U	L	O	C	D	L	R	Q	R
J	E	V	G	F	D	R	K	Z	K	D	Q	A
F	P	I	H	S	R	A	L	O	H	C	S	N
W	Y	T	W	P	B	T	R	G	C	Z	D	I
E	T	A	U	D	A	R	G	G	A	Y	E	M
E	E	R	G	E	D	W	A	S	T	F	Z	E
G	W	X	O	T	H	E	S	I	S	S	C	S
W	E	R	U	T	C	E	L	A	D	J	O	W
S	I	K	T	U	T	O	R	I	A	L	K	P
B	Y	F	Y	T	L	U	C	A	F	N	C	E

degree	scholarship
faculty	seminar
graduate	thesis
literacy	tutorial
postgraduate	undergraduate

Unit 15: Crime

Match the words in column A with the definitions in column B.

A	B
(1) lawyer	(a) not responsible for a crime
(2) innocent	(b) a person who broke the law or did something wrong
(3) alibi	(c) a general term for person who works in and knows about the law
(4) culprit	(d) a reason or evidence that proves you could not have committed a crime

A	B
(1) jury	(a) a place where it is decided if someone is innocent or guilty
(2) judge (n.)	(b) the person who is in charge in a courtroom
(3) barrister (BE)	(c) a lawyer who defends people in court
(4) court (n.)	(d) a group of ordinary people in court who are presented with the facts of a case and decide if people are innocent or guilty

A	B
(1) trial (n.)	(a) a decision made by a judge or jury regarding someone's innocence or guilt
(2) verdict	(b) someone who has suffered from a crime
(3) victim	(c) to formally challenge a decision, especially a verdict, in an attempt to get it changed
(4) appeal (v.)	(d) a process to decide if someone is innocent or guilty

A	B
(1) ban (v.)	(a) illegal
(2) sentence (n.)	(b) punishment by death for a serious crime
(3) capital punishment	(c) a decision by a judge regarding the punishment after someone has been found guilty of a crime
(4) against the law	(d) to not allow/forbid something

A	B
(1) get away with something	(a) to get away from someone or something
(2) weapon	(b) when someone commits a crime and is not caught or is found innocent even though they are guilty
(3) escape from something/someone	(c) an object, such as a gun or knife, used to hurt or kill someone
(4) arrest someone	(d) when the police take someone to a police station on the suspicion of having committed a crime.

A	B
(1) commit a crime	(a) a punishment which involves helping in the community
(2) community service	(b) a person qualified to give legal advice
(3) solicitor (BE)	(c) the person in court accused of committing a crime.
(4) defendant	(d) to do something wrong/break the law

Complete the sentences below with a word from this unit. You may have to change the form of the word so that it fits into the sentence grammatically.

1. I'm sure he killed her, but he was found not guilty. He _____ _____ _____ murder.
2. The _____ announced that the defendant was guilty and sentenced her to three years in jail.
3. The _____ lasted for six months, after which the defendant was found not guilty.
4. He couldn't have committed the crime as he was at his English class at the time. That's a really good _____.
5. The members of the _____ couldn't agree, and it took them three days to reach a verdict about the defendant's innocence or guilt.
6. The police _____ the man on suspicion of stealing the money and took him to the police station for questioning.
7. The criminal had to do three months' _____ _____. His punishment was to pick up litter.
8. She wasn't happy with the verdict so she decided _____ _____.
9. The murder _____ was a gun. The victim was shot in the head.
10. In the U.K., smoking is _____ in all public places. For example, you can't smoke in bars and restaurants.
11. Most of us are a _____ of a crime at some time in our lives. Bad things happen to people all the time.
12. The prisoners _____ from the prison by climbing over the prison walls.

What can you remember?

Now, try to memorise the 24 words in this unit in two minutes. Then, without looking, write down all the words that you can remember.

Crime Vocabulary Word Search

Find the words listed below the word search. They may be vertical, horizontal, diagonal, forwards or backwards. Have fun!

J	L	M	M	K	N	J	P	E	H	Y	T	T
D	L	V	D	Q	I	O	T	X	A	N	C	L
Q	I	E	Q	H	K	T	Q	T	A	R	A	V
D	N	C	J	H	E	X	C	D	R	W	N	M
B	N	R	U	Z	H	U	N	V	Y	U	U	T
S	O	J	R	A	L	E	P	E	R	F	O	R
D	C	I	Y	P	F	S	R	U	V	R	X	C
N	E	W	R	E	T	C	I	D	R	E	V	P
O	N	I	D	X	K	X	E	B	B	I	U	M
X	T	Q	Q	S	O	L	I	C	I	T	O	R
V	Z	R	E	T	S	I	R	R	A	B	U	R
J	L	G	X	X	U	C	F	O	C	B	G	L
I	H	B	E	C	N	E	T	N	E	S	H	L

barrister	jury
court	lawyer
culprit	sentence
defendant	solicitor
innocent	verdict

79

Unit 16: Environment

Match the words in column A with the definitions in column B.

A	B
(1) biodiversity	(a) a disaster
(2) catastrophe	(b) the number and variety of living things in a particular place
(3) climate	(c) to pollute or make impure
(4) contaminate	(d) the regular weather conditions that occur in a particular area

A	B
(1) die out	(a) all the living and non-living things in a particular place and their interactions with each other
(2) ecosystem	(b) the polluting gases emitted from an engine (for example, a car)
(3) endangered	(c) in danger of becoming extinct
(4) exhaust fumes	(d) become extinct

A	B
(1) recycle	(a) things that live in the sea
(2) green	(b) friendly toward the environment
(3) marine life	(c) convert waste, such as paper, glass, and plastic into something that can be used again
(4) fossil fuels	(d) sources of energy, such as coal and oil, formed from the remains of plants and animals which have been dead for a long time

A	B
(1) fracking	(a) a danger
(2) threat	(b) natural energy from the sun, wind, etc. that will always be available
(3) renewable energy	(c) protect something so that it doesn't die out
(4) conserve	(d) a controversial way of extracting fossil fuels from rock

A	B
(1) drought	(a) no longer in existence
(2) sewage	(b) a long period without rain/water
(3) extinct	(c) waste products carried in water
(4) greenhouse effect	(d) what happens when gases get trapped in the atmosphere, warming up the earth

A	B
(1) ozone layer	(a) a layer in the stratosphere protecting life from the sun's radiation
(2) global warming	(b) a fog or haze caused by air pollution
(3) climate change	(c) an increase in temperatures caused by increases in carbon dioxide and methane
(4) smog	(d) changes in the climate – currently used to refer to those changes caused by human activity

Complete the sentences below with a word from this unit. You may have to change the form of the word so that it fits into the sentence grammatically.

1. The hole in the _____ _____ is getting bigger. As a result, more people are getting skin cancer.
2. More and more species are _____ _____. For example, it is thought that there are only about 3,200 tigers left in the world; the rest are thought to be extinct.
3. In order to protect the environment, we must reduce our reliance on _____ _____, such as coal and gas.
4. In some cities in China the _____ is so bad that you can barely see things 100 metres away.
5. If you go snorkelling, you can see that the corals have been damaged by global warming, pollution, and the practice of dynamite fishing. Although you can see plenty of other _____ _____, it too is being affected by these factors.
6. One of the causes of pollution is _____ _____ from cars, lorries and motorcycles.
7. The _____ in England is much colder and wetter than in Egypt.
8. Global warming causes sea levels to rise and is, therefore, a _____ to low lying areas near the coast, which could become flooded.
9. People are trying to be more _____, as they are worried about the environment.
10. Untreated _____ is often pumped straight into the sea and has an adverse effect on marine life.
11. Due to _____ _____, droughts and flooding are becoming more common in some areas, while other areas are experiencing much hotter or colder temperatures than in the recent past.
12. If we _____ more bottles and paper it will have a beneficial effect on the environment, as there will be less waste to dispose of.

What can you remember?

Now, try to memorise the 24 words in this unit in two minutes. Then, without looking, write down all the words that you can remember.

Environment Vocabulary Word Search

Find the words listed below the word search. They may be vertical, horizontal, diagonal, forwards or backwards. Have fun!

O	D	I	V	C	B	F	S	C	N	Q	I	V
G	S	X	M	V	E	S	J	Y	Y	E	W	B
A	B	M	D	P	V	V	R	C	T	H	S	K
O	Q	G	F	Q	M	Z	T	O	I	P	G	D
F	Y	S	P	I	E	P	D	N	S	O	S	E
R	G	C	B	R	T	M	E	T	R	R	E	R
A	D	O	K	M	S	T	W	A	E	T	W	E
C	R	N	J	R	Y	Q	F	M	V	S	A	G
K	O	S	M	Q	S	U	R	I	I	A	G	N
I	U	E	S	M	O	G	Q	N	D	T	E	A
N	G	R	W	X	C	Y	W	A	O	A	T	D
G	H	V	X	V	E	X	G	T	I	C	Z	N
M	T	E	U	X	H	U	Z	E	B	P	U	E

biodiversity	ecosystem
catastrophe	endangered
conserve	fracking
contaminate	sewage
drought	smog

Stop and Check: Units 13–16

Under each paragraph, write the words from the appropriate unit that correspond with the numbered phrases in bold.

Advertising

Advertising takes many forms. Many companies place ¹**advertisements for their products on television or the radio,** for example. They will be helped by ²**another company which specialises in helping companies advertise their products.** They will devise a ³**strategy that helps them advertise their products in the most effective way.** The company will have a ⁴**recogniseable name associated with it.** Some companies might also have a ⁵**catchy phrase** or a ⁶**short, catchy tune** that is associated with their products or with the company itself, or a ⁷**symbol that people associate with them.** Finally, on a personal level, we can all ⁸**advertise things that we own and want to sell in newspapers or on the internet.**

1. _____   5. _____
2. _____   6. _____
3. _____   7. _____
4. _____   8. _____

Education

Most children go to their ¹**first school between the ages of about five and 11.** Here, they learn ²**how to read and write** as well as basic numeracy skills. From about 11 years old until they are about 18, they attend ³**the final years of their schooling,** before getting a job or ⁴**going to university or a similar higher institution of study.** At university, ⁵**the students studying for their first degree** have to attend ⁶**talks given by university lecturers,** and usually take notes. When they ⁷**successfully complete the required coursework and pass their exams,** they can continue their studies by taking a higher degree. ⁸**People who are studying for a higher degree** usually do a Master's degree or Ph.D. Studies have found that the more education a person has, the more money they will earn in their lifetime.

1. _____   5. _____
2. _____   6. _____
3. _____   7. _____
4. _____   8. _____

Crime

Most of us have been ¹**directly affected by a crime** at some point in our lives. Some crimes, however, are more serious than others, especially those involving a ²**gun or**

a knife. All victims hope the perpetrators of the crime they were involved in are caught and charged with the crime. Once a person has been charged with a crime, they go to court, where [3]**the process of deciding whether they are innocent or guilty** takes place. If they don't agree with the [4]**decision relating to their innocence or guilt,** they can [5]**challenge it to try to get it changed.** For committing very serious offences, [6]**people can be executed.** For less serious offences, the criminal might have to [7]**help in the community in some way.** Unfortunately, some people who break the law [8]**never get caught,** while others who have committed no crime are wrongly found guilty.

1. _____   5. _____
2. _____   6. _____
3. _____   7. _____
4. _____   8. _____

Environment

People are becoming more and more concerned about the environment, partly because of [1]**dramatic changes in the weather.** The earth is getting warmer as [2]**gases that are trapped in the atmosphere heat up the planet.** In addition, some areas are [3]**experiencing long periods without rain.** We are also polluting the atmosphere by pumping [4]**untreated human waste** into our rivers and seas. The [5]**things that live in the sea** are being adversely affected by this, as well as by global warming, which is increasing the temperature of the seawater. The use of [6]**energy derived from dead plants and animals** is also harming the environment. In the future, we will have to take measures such as [7]**using products again instead of throwing them away,** so that we no longer [8]**pollute** the environment.

1. _____   5. _____
2. _____   6. _____
3. _____   7. _____
4. _____   8. _____

Unit 17: Geography

Match the words in column A with the definitions in column B.

A	B
(1) peninsula	(a) an area with a lot of towns/cities close together
(2) conurbation	(b) the wide part of a river where it flows into the sea
(3) estuary/mouth	(c) the top of a mountain
(4) peak/summit	(d) a thin strip of land surrounded on three sides by water

A	B
(1) iceberg	(a) an gigantic piece of ice floating in the ocean or sea
(2) canyon	(b) a natural or artificial lake that supplies water for domestic consumption or use in industry
(3) glacier	(c) a large, slowly moving river of ice
(4) reservoir	(d) a deep valley made of rock that was carved out by a river over a long period of time

A	B
(1) boulder	(a) how high something is above sea-level
(2) altitude	(b) the area around the South Pole
(3) Arctic	(c) the area around the North Pole
(4) Antarctic	(d) an extremely large rock

A	B
(1) cartographer	(a) one of the two halves of the earth divided by the equator (northern and southern)
(2) continent (n.)	(b) how far a place is north or south of the equator, measured in degrees
(3) hemisphere	(c) one of the main land masses on the earth, for example Asia, Europe and Africa
(4) latitude	(d) a person who makes maps

A	B
(1) longitude	(a) how far a place is east or west of Greenwich, London, U.K., measured in degrees.
(2) mountain range	(b) an area with lots of small, rounded mountains
(3) hilly	(c) a line of mountains that are more or less connected
(4) rugged	(d) ground having an uneven and rocky terrain

A	B
(1) mound (n.)	(a) a hill with a flat, vertical surface, usually located near the edge of the sea
(2) cliff	(b) a narrow, steep-sided valley
(3) gorge (n.)	(c) a very small river
(4) brook	(d) a small hill

Complete the sentences below with a word from this unit. You may have to change the form of the word so that it fits into the sentence grammatically.

1. The UK is in the northern _____, whereas Australia is in the southern _____.

2. The Andes in South America is the longest _____ _____ in the world.

3. London is situated at approximately 51 degrees _____ north and zero degrees _____.

4. Most penguins can be found in the _____, although they can be found elsewhere in the southern hemisphere, namely in Australia and off the coasts of South America and South Africa.

5. Although England doesn't really have any large mountains, some areas are quite _____.

6. If you climb a mountain too quickly you can get _____ sickness.

7. The Titanic sank during its maiden voyage to New York because it hit an _____ floating in the Atlantic Ocean.

8. Asia is the largest of the seven _____.

9. A large number of people die trying to climb to the _____ of Mt. Everest.

10. A _____ stores water and supplies it to people's homes and local industries.

11. There are many small fish in the _____ near the school.

12. One of the largest _____ in China is the area between Guangzhou and Hong Kong. Millions of people live there.

What can you remember?

Now, try to memorise the 24 words in this unit in two minutes. Then, without looking, write down all the words that you can remember.

Geography Vocabulary Word Search

Find the words listed below the word search. They may be vertical, horizontal, diagonal, forwards or backwards. Have fun!

S	E	A	F	C	E	Y	D	W	U	M	M	K
Y	S	E	Z	B	V	C	F	N	S	Y	D	G
L	T	H	S	O	M	A	A	K	U	S	K	O
R	U	A	A	U	V	R	S	C	L	O	Q	Q
G	A	O	U	L	Q	T	D	P	Q	H	M	O
L	R	S	F	D	H	O	U	E	D	J	T	G
A	Y	B	F	E	V	G	N	N	G	R	E	B
C	I	S	I	R	L	R	W	I	L	G	W	T
I	V	W	L	K	X	A	E	N	D	B	U	J
E	H	W	C	V	C	P	G	S	W	O	N	R
R	G	U	G	J	W	H	R	U	M	O	G	Y
H	F	T	D	X	F	E	O	L	Y	T	K	C
C	A	N	Y	O	N	R	G	A	O	Q	D	B

boulder	glacier
canyon	gorge
cartographer	mound
cliff	peninsula
estuary	rugged

89

Unit 18: Health and Medicine

Match the words in column A with the definitions in column B.

A	B
(1) amputation	(a) resulting in death
(2) fatal	(b) quick to become serious or severe, but lasting only a short time
(3) immune system	(c) the parts of the body that fight diseases and viruses
(4) acute	(d) when a part of the body is removed (e.g. an arm or a leg) in a medical procedure

A	B
(1) chronic	(a) not having enough water in your body
(2) dehydrated	(b) not harmful
(3) benign	(c) the initial treatment people receive when they suffer an injury
(4) first aid	(d) lasting a long time

A	B
(1) hypochondriac	(a) a treatment for cancer using high-energy x-rays
(2) radiotherapy	(b) a person who always imagines they are ill even when they are not
(3) diagnosis	(c) when someone suffers from a loss of mental faculties, such as memory; it usually affects older people.
(4) dementia	(d) a medical explanation of an illness

A	B
(1) germ	(a) the unwanted, bad effects of taking a medicine
(2) transplant (v.)	(b) expected to grow and get worse, probably resulting in death
(3) malignant	(c) to take an organ, for example a kidney, from one person and put it into someone else's body
(4) side-effects	(d) a microorganism that causes disease or sickness

A	B
(1) prescription	(a) a dangerous, microscopic organism that causes the spread of diseases
(2) paralysed	(b) a written piece of paper that indicates the correct type and amount of medicine that you need and how often you should take it, according to a doctor
(3) virus	(c) an injury to the body, especially to the skin
(4) wound (n.)	(d) being unable to move or feel all or a part of the body

A	B
(1) surgeon	(a) the outward sign of an illness
(2) amnesia	(b) a type of treatment for cancer using chemicals that are injected into the body
(3) symptom	(c) a doctor who specialises in performing operations
(4) chemotherapy	(d) a loss of memory

Complete the sentences below with a word from this unit. You may have to change the form of the word so that it fits into the sentence grammatically.

1. The _____ - _____ of the medication include vomiting and diarrhoea.
2. You need to take the _____ to the pharmacy to get the medication. In some countries you can't buy some drugs from the pharmacy without one.
3. Because of a chronic heart problem, he needed to have a heart _____. Now he has a new heart.
4. The car accident left her completely _____. She can't move any part of her body other than her head.
5. If you don't drink enough water, you will become _____.
6. He had a nasty _____ after being shot in the leg. He will have a scar on his leg for the rest of his life.
7. After the accident, he was suffering from _____. He couldn't even remember his own name.
8. The gunshot wound proved to be _____. The woman died shortly after being shot.
9. The _____ of flu include a runny nose, a sore throat and a headache.
10. A large number of old people suffer from _____. It particularly affects their memory.
11. The patient was relieved that the tumour was _____. It was not cancerous as she had feared.
12. It is important to wash your hands in order to prevent the spread of _____.

What can you remember?

Now, try to memorise the 24 words in this unit in two minutes. Then, without looking, write down all the words that you can remember.

Health and Medicine Vocabulary Word Search

Find the words listed below the word search. They may be vertical, horizontal, diagonal, forwards or backwards. Have fun!

T	B	B	T	H	N	L	U	J	Y	K	C	P
C	F	C	N	Y	O	D	M	T	P	D	I	T
H	X	A	A	P	P	M	D	I	A	Q	N	R
E	G	M	N	O	G	E	E	U	R	H	O	A
M	S	P	G	C	R	G	S	G	E	L	R	D
O	U	U	I	H	U	Y	I	N	H	V	H	O
T	R	T	L	O	S	S	S	Y	T	S	C	M
H	I	A	A	N	H	Q	O	E	O	T	G	O
E	V	T	M	D	K	V	N	G	I	J	E	R
R	M	I	L	R	W	I	G	V	D	R	T	T
A	Q	O	B	I	U	E	A	D	A	F	U	G
P	J	N	E	A	Z	Q	I	F	R	M	C	T
Y	W	S	H	C	L	X	D	A	Q	N	A	K

acute	hypochondriac
amputation	malignant
chemotherapy	radiotherapy
chronic	surgeon
diagnosis	virus

93

Unit 19: Science and Technology

Match the words in column A with the definitions in column B.

A	B
(1) gadget	(a) to make something better/to get closer to completing something
(2) make progress	(b) a small device/invention, usually novel and ingenious
(3) nanotechnology	(c) the science/technology of working with very small things
(4) geek/nerd	(d) a person obsessed with technology who some people consider to be boring and socially inept

A	B
(1) state-of-the-art	(a) to show how something is done
(2) outdated	(b) a scientific procedure undertaken to discover something new
(3) demonstrate	(c) the latest/newest model/technology
(4) experiment (n.)	(d) referring to technology that is no longer new or in fashion

A	B
(1) innovation	(a) knowing how to use computers
(2) high-tech	(b) to arrange things according to their type/category
(3) classify	(c) the introduction of new things or methods
(4) computer-literate	(d) using or requiring the latest technology

A	B
(1) microchip	(a) a prefix denoting that something is related to computers or the internet
(2) develop	(b) a very small but important part of many electronic devices
(3) 'cyber-'	(c) the very latest technology, research, design etc.
(4) cutting-edge	(d) to make something more advanced or effective

A	B
(1) obsolete	(a) out-of-date and no longer in use
(2) labour-saving	(b) a person who is afraid of technology
(3) research (v.)	(c) reducing the amount of work or effort needed
(4) technophobe	(d) to investigate and study something to find out new things

A	B
(1) breakthrough	(a) the study or use of computers or other electronic equipment to send/store information
(2) hypothesis/theory	(b) a sudden and important discovery
(3) information technology(IT)	(c) a programme that helps you find information on the internet
(4) search engine	(d) an idea that needs to be tested to see if it is true

Complete the sentences below with a word from this unit. You may have to change the form of the word so that it fits into the sentence grammatically.

1. The washing machine is a great _____ - _____ device. Before its invention, it could take hours to wash all your clothes.
2. I'm a _____. I hate technology.
3. He was mad about computers so he decided to study _____ _____ at university.
4. I've got the latest iPhone. It's amazing! It's really _____ _____ _____ _____. It uses all the latest technology.
5. The old Nokia phone that our teacher has is really _____.
6. As part of her Master's degree, the student did some _____ into how people learn a second language.
7. The teacher _____ how to conduct the experiment. The students then did it themselves.
8. If you want to get a good job you have to be _____ - _____, as if you can't use computers you won't get a very good job.
9. The polio vaccine was a great scientific _____, as it virtually eliminated the disease worldwide.
10. You can use a _____ _____ to find information on the internet.
11. He's such a _____. All he is interested in is computers.
12. Video cameras are virtually _____. Nobody uses them anymore, as other more advanced technology has replaced them.

What can you remember?

Now, try to memorise the 24 words in this unit in two minutes. Then, without looking, write down all the words that you can remember.

Science and Technology Vocabulary Word Search

Find the words listed below the word search. They may be vertical, horizontal, diagonal, forwards or backwards. Have fun!

W	M	I	C	R	O	C	H	I	P	A	J	B
I	A	E	F	W	C	L	A	S	S	I	F	Y
O	R	P	T	Q	Y	W	L	P	T	K	G	P
T	E	P	J	F	X	B	D	G	U	V	W	S
B	B	R	E	A	K	T	H	R	O	U	G	H
C	U	T	T	I	N	G	E	D	G	E	Q	U
M	A	K	E	P	R	O	G	R	E	S	S	U
C	P	O	L	E	V	E	D	W	J	L	E	M
D	K	F	T	D	D	G	W	H	P	E	J	E
P	G	K	T	N	E	M	I	R	E	P	X	E
Q	Q	K	E	O	C	T	E	G	D	A	G	N
V	S	I	S	E	H	T	O	P	Y	H	O	T
F	I	E	H	N	G	Y	Y	C	V	C	B	P

breakthrough	gadget
classify	geek
cutting edge	hypothesis
develop	make progress
experiment	microchip

97

Unit 20: Work

Match the words in A with the definitions in B.

A	B
(1) employee	(a) to lose your job because you are no longer needed by your employer; to be laid off
(2) employer	(b) someone who works for someone else
(3) resign/quit	(c) someone who/a company that has other people that work for him/her/it
(4) made redundant (BE)	(d) to tell your employer that you no longer want to work for them

A	B
(1) overtime	(a) an occupation that requires training and formal qualifications
(2) flexitime	(b) to lose your job because you've done something wrong
(3) sacked/fired	(c) time worked in addition to your normal hours
(4) profession	(d) a system where you do not have fixed start and finish times when working, but start and finish when you want, while still working the same total number of hours per week/month

A	B
(1) unemployed (adj.)	(a) a person learning to do a job
(2) trainee	(b) without a job when you are in need of one
(3) wage	(c) the type of job you have
(4) occupation	(d) the amount of money you earn (normally per hour or per week)

A	B
(1) CV (curriculum vitae)	(a) information about your education, past employment, etc. used when applying for a job
(2) shift-work	(b) to work irregular hours (different hours on different days)
(3) salary	(c) to work about 40 hours a week
(4) full-time job	(d) the amount of money you earn (normally per year)

A	B
(1) intern	(a) a young person who is working somewhere to get experience and is not getting paid for that work
(2) apprentice	(b) time off work given to women who have just had a baby
(3) qualifications	(c) a person learning how to do a job from someone who is skilled at doing it
(4) maternity leave	(d) the education or experience you have that make you suitable for a particular job

A	B
(1) CEO (Chief Executive Officer)	(a) money you get from the government if you are not working
(2) hand in your notice	(b) to stop working as a protest about something you don't like about your job or employer
(3) unemployment benefit	(c) to tell your employer you no longer want to work for them
(4) go on strike	(d) the person with the most important job in a company

Complete the sentences below with a word from this unit. You may have to change the form of the word so that it fits into the sentence grammatically.

1. She has a fantastic _____. She gets $1,000,000 a year.
2. I used to do _____. On some days, I would work from 2 p.m. to 10 p.m., while on others I would work from 6 a.m. to 2 p.m.
3. In the UK if you are not working, you get _____ _____ from the government, which helps you to get by until you find another job.
4. When you apply for a job, you should send your _____ _____ along with a covering letter. This should include information about your education and work experience.
5. Being a doctor is a worthwhile _____, as you can earn a reasonable amount of money and help people who are sick or injured.
6. As I am a student, I don't have time to do a _____ _____ job. I do, however, have a part-time job.
7. Working _____ is great because it means that if I don't want to, I don't have to get up early in the morning and can start and finish work when I like.
8. I will get paid a lot more this month, as I've done lots of _____ in addition to my normal hours.
9. My friend is an _____ at a bank. He doesn't get paid, but he is getting a lot of good work experience.
10. Owing to the decrease in demand for the product, a large proportion of the workforce was _____ _____.
11. The worker's went _____ _____ in order to get more money.
12. I didn't like my job much. After having an argument with my boss, I decided to _____ _____ _____ _____.

What can you remember?

Now, try to memorise the 24 words in this unit in two minutes. Then, without looking, write down all the words that you can remember.

Work Vocabulary Word Search

Find the words listed below the word search. They may be vertical, horizontal, diagonal, forwards or backwards. Have fun!

T	E	D	Q	K	J	E	E	F	B	N	E	L
W	D	M	O	O	U	H	W	G	O	S	M	F
G	D	S	I	N	X	H	U	I	A	W	A	F
Q	O	E	J	T	H	S	S	U	L	W	A	T
J	O	A	Y	V	I	S	N	V	A	P	J	E
E	S	K	D	O	E	X	W	M	P	K	T	N
M	M	B	K	F	L	T	E	R	T	R	K	G
P	W	P	O	N	E	P	E	L	A	O	T	I
L	P	R	L	I	L	N	M	I	F	Q	W	S
O	P	Y	P	O	T	L	N	E	V	T	I	E
Y	U	V	N	I	Y	E	A	W	N	P	A	R
E	X	G	C	D	E	E	I	N	F	U	N	F
R	D	E	K	C	A	S	E	K	S	X	B	B

apprentice	resign
employee	sacked
employer	trainee
flexitime	unemployed
profession	wage

Stop and Check: Units 17–20

Under each paragraph, write the words from the appropriate unit that correspond with the numbered phrases in bold.

Geography

The landscape around the world varies considerably. Some areas are flat, while others have a [1]**large number of mountains in the same area that form a chain.** Some mountains, such as Mt. Everest, are very high, and it is necessary to take precautions when climbing them because of the great [2]**height above sea level,** which can cause sickness. Other [3]**areas have mountains that are small and rounded in appearance.** There are large rivers such as the Nile and [4]**very small rivers only a couple of meters wide.** [5]**Rivers get much bigger where they meet the sea,** of course. [6]**People who make maps** have shown these features on the maps, as well as [7]**how far places are from the equator** and [8]**how far they are from a place near London called Greenwich.**

1.	_____	5.	_____
2.	_____	6.	_____
3.	_____	7.	_____
4.	_____	8.	_____

Health and Medicine

If we are sick, we usually go to a doctor. They will tell us [1]**what they think we are suffering from.** They will often tell us [2]**what medicine we need to take and how often we need to take it.** It is possible that the medicine will have some [3]**unwanted negative effects.** For more serious conditions, we might have to go to hospital and be operated on by a [4]**doctor who performs operations.** It is possible that they might have to [5]**remove a part of our body and replace it with the same part from another person.** Most illnesses can be treated and are not [6]**likely to result in death.** Some illnesses, however, [7]**last a long time.** All of us worry about our health, but some [8]**people imagine that they are ill even when they are not.** The best thing we can do is live a healthy lifestyle, eat healthy food and get plenty of sleep and exercise. As the saying goes, "Prevention is better than cure."

1.	_____	5.	_____
2.	_____	6.	_____
3.	_____	7.	_____
4.	_____	8.	_____

Science and Technology

Over the last 50 years, technology has changed our lives dramatically. Lots of [1]**clever electronic devices** have made our lives more interesting, and appliances like washing machines and dishwashers [2]**have reduced the amount of work we have to do.** Some [3]**people who are obsessed with technology** spend all their time with computers. The rest of us, while not obsessed with it, are still heavily dependent on technology. We all want the [4]**latest and most up-to-date** phone, for example, because the one we bought a few years ago is now [5]**no longer up-to-date.** Today, it is necessary [6]**to have a good knowledge of computers** in order to get a good job as they are now commonly used in most workplaces. Devices that are very sophisticated and [7]**use a lot of technology** are now a big part of our lives. Not everyone embraces technology, however. There are some [8]**people who hate it and even fear it.**

1. _____
2. _____
3. _____
4. _____
5. _____
6. _____
7. _____
8. _____

Work

All of us want to get a good job. To do so, we need to have [1]**the right education and relevant experience** for the positions we apply for. Most of us work for [2]**other people who employ us,** although some people are self-employed. Similarly, most of us [3]**have a job that requires us to work about 40 hours a week.** If we don't like our job, however, we can [4]**tell the employer that we don't want to work for them anymore.** Conversely, especially during a recession, an employer may tell us that [5]**they don't need us to work for them anymore, as there is not enough work.** We could also [6]**lose our job if we do something our employer doesn't like.** Some people, of course, are [7]**unable to get a job and are not working.** In some countries, the government gives them [8]**money to live on while they are out of work.** The perfect job, of course, is one that we enjoy doing and that pays us enough to live on and also allows us to enjoy the other parts of our lives.

1. _____
2. _____
3. _____
4. _____
5. _____
6. _____
7. _____
8. _____

Test Your Vocabulary Knowledge
Unit 1: Globalisation

- S _ _ _ _ _ a _ _ s _ _ _ _ _ are documents that show that you own part of a company.
- C _ _ _ _ _ _ _ _ _ is the act of buying and then using a product or service.
- A s _ _ _ _ m _ _ _ _ _ is a place where stocks and shares are bought and sold.
- M _ _ _ _ _ _ _ _ _ _ _ _ is the act of making/producing something using machinery.
- T _ _ _ _ b _ _ _ _ _ _ _ are regulations that prevent trade between countries.
- To i _ _ _ _ _ _ _ _ is to arrive in a new country to start a new life.
- A _ _ _ _ _ _ _ _ is possessing abundant wealth.
- I _ _ _ _ _ _ _ _ is a situation where prices increase.
- P _ _ _ _ _ _ _ _ _ _ is a situation where people are making a lot of money and living a good life.
- A t _ _ _ _ _ is a government tax on imports.
- A _ _ _ _ _ _ _ _ _ is the recording and managing of a company's finances.
- O _ _ _ _ _ _ _ _ _ _ is when a company gets another company to do work for it which it could have done itself, often in a foreign country.
- E _ _ _ _ _ _ _ g _ _ _ _ _ is a situation where the economy is getting bigger.
- To i _ _ _ _ _ is to buy goods from another country.
- E _ _ _ _ _ _ _ _ _ is a situation where people leave their country to live abroad.
- To e _ _ _ _ _ _ is to sell goods made in your country to another country.
- T _ _ B _ _ _ _ _ _ o _ T _ _ _ _ is the difference in value between imports and exports in a particular country.
- A r _ _ _ _ _ _ _ _ is a situation where the economy is stagnant or performing badly.
- A s _ _ _ _ _ _ _ _ _ _ is a very powerful country with a very strong military and economy, such as the USA or China, which can influence world events.
- A m _ _ _ _ _ _ _ _ _ _ _ _ _ _ c _ _ _ _ _ _ _ _ _ _ is a company operating in at least one other country outside of its home country.
- A f _ _ _ _ _ _ _ _ is the right to sell a company's goods and/or services in a particular area.
- T _ _ s _ _ _ _ _ _ _ _ o _ l _ _ _ _ _ is how comfortable and wealthy people are in a particular country or area and the value of their possessions.
- T _ _ _ _ _ _ _ is the system of taking money from people by governments to pay for public services like schools, roads, and hospitals and other expenditures.
- M _ _ _ _ _ _ _ _ _ is the action a company takes to try to promote/sell its products and services.

Unit 2: Money and Finance

- A c _ _ _ _ _ _ _ is the type of money used in a particular country.
- The e _ _ _ _ _ _ _ r _ _ _ is the amount of money you get if you change the money of one country's currency into the currency of another country.
- I _ _ _ _ _ _ _ is the extra money you get over time when you save money, or the extra money you have to pay when you borrow money.
- A c _ _ _ _ _ c _ _ _ is a bank card you can use to borrow money, which you then have to repay at a later date.
- The c _ _ _ o _ l _ _ _ _ _ is the average cost of everyday items in a particular area or country.
- A f _ _ is the money you have to pay for some kind of service.
- C _ _ _ is money in the form of notes and coins as opposed to credit or debit cards and such like.
- To i _ _ _ _ _ is to buy something in the hope that it will increase in value in the future, when you can sell it and make a profit, or to put money into a business venture.
- A b _ _ _ l _ _ _ is money you borrow from a bank and repay with interest at a later date.
- B _ _ _ _ _ _ _ means that a company or individual has failed financially and is unable to pay others the money they owe.
- A p _ _ _ _ _ _ is the money you get (from a fund you or your employer have previously paid into while you were working) when you are old and no longer working.
- O _ c _ _ _ _ _ is when you buy something and pay for it at a later date.
- A m _ _ _ _ _ _ _ is the money you borrow to buy a house which you owe the bank and which you must repay to them with interest over a certain amount of time.
- An o _ _ _ _ _ _ _ _ _ is the money you owe the bank because you have taken more money out of your account that you had in it.
- A r _ _ _ _ _ is the money you get back when you have paid too much for something, such as taxes.
- A c _ _ _ _ _ c _ _ _ _ _ is a time when it is difficult to borrow the money from a bank or other places that lend money.
- A d _ _ _ _ _ _ is the money you pay to secure the purchase of something before you pay the full amount at a later date.
- E _ _ _ _ _ _ _ _ _ _ is the money you spend.
- I _ _ _ _ _ t _ _ is the money you have to pay to the government on your earnings.
- The b _ _ _ _ m _ _ _ _ _ is the illegal economy.
- W _ _ _ _ _ _ _ _ means not worth anything or not useful.
- P _ _ _ _ _ _ _ _ means very valuable or precious.
- W _ _ _ o _ _ means wealthy/affluent.
- A d _ _ _ _ c _ _ _ is a bank card you can use to take money out of your bank account.

Unit 3: Food

- A b _ _ _ _ _ _ _ is a drink.
- O _ _ _ _ _ _ _ _ _ means fat/obese.
- C _ _ _ _ _ _ _ _ _ _ _ is a waxy substance in your blood, too much of which can be harmful.
- G _ _ _ _ _ _ _ _ _ _ m _ _ _ _ _ _ _ is when food has been made different in some way by changing its DNA.
- V _ _ _ _ _ _ _ are essential organic compounds the body needs in small amounts to stay healthy.
- A b _ _ _ _ _ _ _ d _ _ _ is when you eat the right amount of different types of food to stay healthy.
- O _ _ _ _ _ _ means to be grown naturally, without the use of artificial fertilizers, pesticides, or chemicals.
- A v _ _ _ _ _ _ _ _ is a person who does not eat meat or fish.
- M _ _ _ _ _ _ _ _ _ _ _ means underfed/not having enough to eat or enough of the right kinds of food which provide the necessary nutrients.
- N _ _ _ _ _ _ _ _ are important substances necessary for good health.
- A s _ _ _ _ is a small amount of food eaten between regular means.
- F _ _ is a greasy solid found in meat and plants that provides energy in your diet; eating too much of it can be harmful.
- A c _ _ _ _ _ _ _ / r _ _ _ _ _ _ _ _ is an eating place at work or university/college.
- O _ _ _ _ _ _ is a situation where people are extremely fat/overweight.
- A c _ _ _ _ _ _ is the amount energy that food will produce; if you eat too many, you will get fat.
- A p _ _ _ _ _ _ is a serving or the amount of a specific food deemed suitable for one person.
- P _ _ _ _ _ _ is a substance found in meat, fish, eggs, and beans which is an essential part of one's diet.
- A c _ _ _ _ _ _ _ _ _ _ _ is a naturally occurring substance found in food that gives you energy.
- C _ _ _ _ _ _ _ _ _ _ _ _ is a collective word for sweets and chocolate.
- F _ _ _ f _ _ _ is food that you can get very quickly such as hamburgers and pizza.
- An a _ _ _ _ _ _ is an intolerance to a particular type of food which causes an adverse reaction when eaten.
- To h _ _ _ a h _ _ _ _ _ _ a _ _ _ _ _ _ _ means to have the desire to eat a good amount of food.
- F _ _ _ p _ _ _ _ _ _ _ _ is when you become sick as a direct result of eating contaminated food.
- M _ _ _ _ _ _ _ are naturally occurring, important substances in food, such as calcium and iron.

Unit 4: Sport and Leisure

- A l _ _ _ _ _ _ _ _ is the sort of life you have and the things you do.
- R _ _ _ _ _ _ _ _ _ _ means related to leisure/your free time.
- A s _ _ _ _ _ l _ _ _ is what you do in your free time that involves other people.
- A c _ _ _ _ p _ _ _ _ _ is a lazy person who sits in front of the television all day and gets very little exercise.
- B _ _ _ _ _ j _ _ _ _ _ _ is an activity where you jump from a very high structure, like a bridge, while attached to a stretchable rubber cord and then bounce up and down.
- S _ _ _ d _ _ _ _ _ is when you swim underwater using special breathing apparatus.
- P _ _ _ _ _ _ _ _ _ _ is an activity which involves jumping off mountains and floating around while attached to a parachute.
- T _ _ _ _ _ _ _ is walking long distances in the countryside or mountains over a period of days or even weeks.
- T _ _ _ _ _ b _ _ _ _ _ _ _ is an activity where you roll a hard rubber or plastic ball down a track in order to knock down skittles.
- S _ _ _ _ _ _ _ _ _ are the people who go to watch an even, especially a sporting event.
- A s _ _ _ _ _ _ is a large building where people go to watch a sporting event.
- A r _ _ _ _ _ _ is a person who watches a game, makes decisions, and penalises players or teams in order to ensure that they follow the rules.
- G _ _ _ _ _ _ _ _ _ is a sport involving complex body movements and special equipment, such as uneven bars and balance beams.
- A r _ _ _ _ _ _ t _ _ _ _ is an artificial surface, usually in the shape of an oval, where athletes can run and compete in sporting events like running races.
- A s _ _ _ _ is a group of people who play a particular sport from whom a team is picked.
- To h _ _ _ a p _ _ _ _ _ is to go to the countryside and eat a pre-packed meal in the open air.
- S _ _ _ _ _ _ _ _ _ means not active or not involving physical activity.
- W _ _ _ - l _ _ _ b _ _ _ _ _ _ is getting the balance right between work and leisure.
- E _ _ _ _ _ _ _ _ _ means related to riding horses.
- A m _ _ _ _ _ _ _ is a very long-distance running race.
- M _ _ _ _ _ _ _ a _ _ _ are various sports which originated in the Far East as forms of self-defence, such as judo,
- To t _ _ _ a s _ _ _ _ _ is to go for a leisurely walk.
- To l _ _ o _ _ s _ _ _ _ is to do an activity to help you relax/unwind.
- A J _ _ _ _ _ _ is a large hot bath with bubbles in it that massages the body.

Unit 5: Politics

- P _ _ _ _ _ _ _ _ means having a great love of your country.
- R _ _ _ _ _ _ is when you think something which is very different from what most people think.
- T _ _ _ _ _ _ _ _ _ _ _ is a system in which there is only one political party, and citizens have no freedom of speech or democratic rights.
- A r _ _ _ _ - w _ _ _ person is a person who strongly believes in capitalism/the free market.
- A l _ _ _ - w _ _ _ person is a person who believes in socialism/equality.
- A c _ _ _ _ _ _ _ _ is a person who is applying for a political position.
- N _ _ _ _ _ _ _ _ _ _ is when the interests of your country are more important than anything else.
- An i _ _ _ _ _ _ _ is a political perspective or way of seeing the world, such as conservatism or communism.
- A _ _ _ _ _ _ _ _ is an ideology that asserts that laws and governments are not important or necessary.
- A c _ _ _ _ _ _ _ _ is an official group of people who need to make decisions about a particular issue.
- A m _ _ _ _ _ _ _ is a form of government in which a king or queen is in charge.
- A m _ _ _ _ _ _ _ is a department of government that is responsible for one particular area of interest, such as education or defence.
- A p _ _ _ _ _ _ _ _ is the head of state in a republic.
- An e _ _ _ _ _ _ _ is when people vote for the person/party that they want to form a government.
- A r _ _ _ _ _ _ _ _ _ is a vote by all the registered voters in a country or area on a particular issue.
- The p _ _ _ _ m _ _ _ _ _ _ _ _ is the most important minister in a government.
- A d _ _ _ _ _ _ _ _ is a system of government where the people have the power to elect a government of their own choosing.
- A p _ _ _ _ _ is a proposal on a particular issue.
- A p _ _ _ _ _ _ _ _ p _ _ _ _ is a group of people who have similar political beliefs and who want to form a government.
- To v _ _ _ in an election is to choose which party you want to form a government.
- A s _ _ _ _ _ _ _ _ is a person who believes in equality and the equal distribution of wealth.
- A c _ _ _ _ _ _ _ _ _ _ _ is a person who believes in preserving traditions.
- A c _ _ _ is when a government is overthrown, usually by the army or armed forces, and is replaced by a new government.
- A c _ _ _ _ _ _ _ _ is when two or more parties work together to govern a country.

Unit 6: Travel and Transport

- An e _ _ _ _ _ _ _ _ is a trip to see a specific a place or thing, made for pleasure.
- A t _ _ _ _ _ _ _ is a building where trains, aircraft, and buses leave and arrive.
- A _ _ - i _ _ _ _ _ _ _ _ is when everything (such as food and drinks) is included in the price of a holiday or hotel.
- A d _ _ _ _ _ is a change in the route you are taking in order to avoid something or see something of interest.
- F _ _ _ _ _ _ _ _ _ are the amenities a hotel or place has, such as a swimming pool, restaurant, etc.
- J _ _ l _ _ is being tired after a long flight caused by the time difference between the country you left and the country you arrived in.
- A c _ _ is another word for a taxi.
- L _ _ _ _ _ a _ _ _ _ _ _ _ _ _ _ _ _ _ is very expensive, comfortable hotels, apartments, etc.
- To c _ _ _ _ - i _ is to register at a hotel or airport.
- E _ _ _ _ _ _ _ _ _ is tourism that is friendly to the environment.
- I _ _ _ _ _ _ _ _ _ _ is the place at an airport where you have to show your passport to officials before you can leave or enter the country.
- A f _ _ _ _ is a boat or ship that goes back and forth between two places, carrying people, cars, or products.
- H _ _ _ l _ _ _ _ _ _ is luggage you carry onto an aircraft yourself.
- A _ _ _ _ _ _ _ refers to anything related to aircraft.
- A d _ _ _ _ _ _ _ _ _ _ is the place you are going to.
- An i _ _ _ _ _ _ _ _ is a list of places you will visit on a tour.
- A j _ _ _ _ _ _ is when you travel from one place to another.
- L _ _ _ - h _ _ _ refers to a flight travelling a long distance, normally between two or more continents.
- A c _ _ _ _ is a man-made river.
- S _ _ _ _ - h _ _ _ refers to a flight travelling a short or medium distance, normally within a country or continent.
- B _ _ _ _ _ a _ _ _ _ _ _ _ _ _ _ _ _ is a very cheap place to stay.
- A t _ _ _ is a journey undertaken, especially one for pleasure.
- To e _ _ _ _ _ _ is to get onto a ship.
- To d _ _ _ _ _ _ _ _ is to get off a ship.

Unit 7: Media

- A p _ _ _ _ _ _ _ _ is the owner of a newspaper.
- To be w _ _ _ - i _ _ _ _ _ _ _ is to know a lot about something.
- A h _ _ _ _ _ _ _ is the main heading at the top of an article or page of a newspaper.
- To b _ _ _ _ _ _ _ is to transmit a programme on radio or television.
- A s _ _ _ _ _ _ _ _ is an object that orbits the earth and transmits or collects information.
- A p _ _ _ _ _ _ _ is a person that prepares a book, magazine, newspaper, or electronic information so that it is ready to be sold.
- J _ _ _ _ _ _ _ _ _ is the process of writing factual information for publication in a newspaper or on the internet or to be broadcast on television or the radio.
- C _ _ _ _ _ _ _ _ _ is when the government places restrictions on what people can say.
- A h _ _ _ _ _ _ _ _ is something that claims to predict your future based on your date of birth and the movement of the stars and planets.
- An e _ _ _ _ _ _ is one part of a series of programmes.
- A p _ _ _ _ _ _ _ _ is a person who hosts /fronts a programme.
- A s _ _ _ _ _ _ _ _ _ _ is an arrangement whereby you pay money in advance to read or watch something over a period of time, such as a particular magazine or satellite channel.
- A t _ _ _ _ _ _ is a small, low-quality newspaper.
- A j _ _ _ _ _ _ is a specialist magazine relating to a particular subject.
- To see an event l _ _ _ is when you see someone, such as actors, musicians, or athletes performing in person as something is happening (not pre-recorded).
- The p _ _ _ _ _ _ _ _ are photographers who take photos of famous people.
- A f _ _ _ p _ _ _ _ is when newspapers and television channels can say whatever they like without censorship.
- P _ _ - p _ _ - v _ _ _ is when you pay to watch a specific event, such as a football match, on television or the internet.
- The e _ _ _ _ _ is the person who decides what a film, book, or newspaper article should include and will eventually look like.
- A r _ _ _ _ _ _ _ is a person who collects and/or reports the news.
- A d _ _ _ _ _ _ _ _ _ is a factual film about a particular topic.
- A s _ _ _ o _ _ _ _ is a television drama series based on the lives of ordinary, but fictional, people.
- C _ _ _ _ _ _ a _ _ _ _ _ _ refers to what is being reported in the news at the present time.
- The p _ _ _ _ is a collective word for newspapers, magazines, and journalists.

Unit 8: Architecture

- To d _ _ _ _ _ _ something, such as a building, is to completely destroy it.
- W _ _ _ - d _ _ _ _ _ _ _ _ means it serves its purpose well or is attractive.
- A b _ _ _ _ _ / s _ _ _ _ _ a _ _ _ _ _ _ _ is an apartment consisting of just one room containing a bed and a living area.
- C _ _ _ _ _ _ is a hard material used in constructing buildings.
- D _ _ _ _ _ _ _ refers to a building which is in very bad condition and is no longer inhabited.
- C _ _ _ _ _ _ _ _ _ _ is the process of building something, like a work or living structure, a road, or a bridge.
- H _ _ _ - r _ _ _ refers to a high, multi-storied building.
- F _ _ _ _ _ _ _ _ _ means very modern, like something might look in the future.
- A d _ _ _ _ _ _ _ h _ _ _ _ is a house that is not attached to another house.
- A b _ _ _ _ _ _ is a platform on the outside of a room on an upper floor of a building that has a low wall or rail around it.
- An e _ _ _ _ _ _ is a very ugly building.
- The s _ _ _ _ _ _ _ _ of a building refers to the way it is constructed using different parts.
- I _ _ _ _ _ _ _ _ _ refers to the materials that are used to stop heat or sound from escaping from a building.
- A s _ _ _ is a poor area containing very poor-quality housing.
- A c _ _ _ _ _ _ is a small house in the country.
- M _ _ _ _ _ _ _ _ refers to a style that is very different from traditional or conventional styles.
- A c _ _ _ _ _ is a pillar that supports the structure of a building.
- A s _ _ _ _ _ _ _ _ _ is a very high, multi-storied building.
- A p _ _ _ _ is a flat outside area with a stone or concrete floor adjoining a house where people can sit to relax.
- L _ _ - r _ _ _ refers to a low building, often with only one or two stories.
- A s _ _ _ _ _ (BE)/s _ _ _ _ (AE) is a level or floor of a building.
- A g _ _ _ _ c _ _ _ _ _ _ _ _ is a collection of houses in an area surrounded by a security wall with a guarded entrance.
- A c _ _ _ _ e _ _ _ _ _ _ _ is a person who designed and helps construct roads, bridges, etc.
- A t _ _ _ _ _ _ is a paved area outside a building, similar to a patio.

Unit 9: Town and Country

- A s _ _ _ _ _ _ _ m _ _ _ is a very large building containing many shops, restaurants, and the like inside.
- C _ _ _ _ are plants that are grown in large quantities to be eaten.
- D _ _ _ _ _ _ _ _ _ _ _ is when the number of people living in an area is getting smaller.
- I _ _ _ _ _ _ _ _ _ is the artificial supply of water for crops.
- R _ _ _ _ refers to the countryside.
- A h _ _ _ _ _ _ e _ _ _ _ _ is an area with a lot of similar houses together.
- A _ _ _ _ _ l _ _ _ is agricultural land used to grow crops.
- A f _ _ _ _ _ _ _ _ _ is a substance, often consisting of chemicals, used on the land in order to increase the amount of crops grown. A m _ _ _ _ _ _ _ is a really big city, usually with a population of more than 10 million people.
- P _ _ _ _ _ t _ _ _ _ _ _ _ _ is transport that everyone can use, such as buses and trains.
- C _ _ _ _ _ _ _ _ _ _ _ _ refers to a situation where there are many people from different countries and cultures living in the same area.
- An o _ _ _ _ _ b _ _ _ _ is a large, high building containing offices.
- T _ _ _ _ _ _ c _ _ _ _ _ _ _ _ _ is when there is too much traffic in one place.
- I _ _ _ _ _ _ _ _ _ _ _ _ _ refers to the basic facilities in an area, such as bridges, roads, and sewage systems that are necessary for a society to function properly.
- U _ _ _ _ is a word used to refer to a town/city.
- B _ _ _ _ _ _ are poor people who ask you to give them money.
- M _ _ _ _ _ _ _ _ _ _ _ is a word which is used to refer to a large town/city and the surrounding area.
- U _ _ _ _ s _ _ _ _ _ is when an urban area starts spreading out and taking over areas of countryside.
- The o _ _ _ _ _ _ _ _ of a town/city are the areas around its edges.
- A p _ _ _ _ _ _ _ _ _ p _ _ _ _ _ _ _ is an area, normally containing shops and restaurants where motorised traffic is banned and people can walk freely.
- T _ _ r _ _ _ h _ _ _ is a time when the roads are unusually busy because people are travelling to and from work.
- The s _ _ _ _ _ _ are an area, often residential, away from the centre of a town/city.
- I _ _ _ _ c _ _ _ refers to the central parts of a city.
- O _ _ _ _ _ _ _ _ _ _ _ is when there are too many people in one place.

Unit 10: Family

- A s _ _ _ _ _ _ _ _ / s _ _ _ _ _ _ _ _ is the person your father or mother marries after your biological parents have divorced or one of them has died.
- A _ _ _ _ _ _ _ _ are people related to us who lived a long time before we did.
- A w _ _ _ _ / w _ _ _ _ _ _ is a woman/man whose husband/wife has died.
- R _ _ _ _ _ _ _ _ are people who are related to you who are still alive.
- A b _ _ _ _ _ _ _ is a man who has never been married.
- To d _ _ _ _ _ _ is to separate and no longer be legally be married.
- T _ _ e _ _ _ _ _ _ is a polite way of referring to old people.
- O _ _ _ _ _ _ _ _ are a person's child/children or the young of an animal.
- An e _ _ _ _ _ _ _ _ _ is an arrangement between two people to marry each other in the future.
- J _ _ _ _ _ _ _ is a word which refers to young people or means immature.
- A g _ _ _ _ _ _ _ is an adult who is responsible for a young person who is not their biological child.
- An e _ _ _ _ _ _ _ f _ _ _ _ _ is a family which includes relatives that are not closely related, such as uncles, aunts, and their children.
- An a _ _ _ _ _ _ _ _ _ is a teenager who is almost an adult.
- M _ _ _ _ _ _ _ is a word which refers to things that have to do with mothers.
- A n _ _ _ _ _ _ f _ _ _ _ _ is a family unit consisting of only parents and their children.
- The b _ _ _ _ _ _ _ _ _ _ is the person who earns the most money in the family
- P _ _ _ _ _ _ _ is a word which refers to things that have to do with fathers.
- A g _ _ _ _ _ _ _ _ is a very old person, especially one suffering from poor health.
- A _ _ _ _ _ _ _ _ is the legal process of becoming a parent of a child who is not your own.
- A s _ _ _ _ _ c _ _ _ _ _ _ is an old person who is probably no longer working.
- U _ _ _ _ _ _ _ _ _ refers to how children are raised, educated, and nurtured.
- G _ _ _ _ are units of heredity which are passed from parents to their children.
- S _ _ _ _ _ _ _ are brothers or sisters.
- An a _ _ _ _ _ _ _ m _ _ _ _ _ _ _ is when parents decide who their children will marry.

Unit 11: Social Issues

- D _ _ _ _ _ _ _ _ _ _ _ _ _ is when you treat people differently for unfair reasons, such as the colour of their skin or their gender.
- A _ _ _ _ _ _ _ _ _ _ are the basic rights that animals should have, such as not being used for medical research or hunted.
- A r _ _ _ _ _ _ is a person who has had to leave their country for political reasons or to escape from a war or natural disaster.
- T _ _ _ _ _ _ _ _ is organised violence used to frighten people for political purposes.
- H _ _ _ _ _ _ _ _ _ _ are the basic rights that all people should have.
- P _ _ _ _ _ _ _ _ _ _ _ _ is the permission to live in another country because you are being persecuted in your own country.
- A d _ _ _ _ _ _ _ _ is a person who disagrees with the government of their country.
- An o _ _ _ _ _ _ is a person who does not fit into the society they live in because they are different in some way and is often shunned.
- E _ _ _ _ _ c _ _ _ _ _ _ _ _ is when members of a particular race are killed to eliminate them from a particular area.
- C _ _ _ _ r _ _ _ _ _ refer to the rights of people in a society.
- A s _ _ _ _ _ _ _ is a person who lives in an unoccupied building without paying rent.
- R _ _ _ _ _ is when you treat someone differently because of their race or skin colour.
- G _ _ _ _ _ _ _ _ is the killing of a large number of people, often because of their race.
- An a _ _ _ _ _ _ _ is when a pregnancy is deliberately terminated.
- H _ _ _ _ _ _ _ _ _ _ _ is the situation that exists when people don't have a particular home to live in.
- An e _ _ _ _ _ _ m _ _ _ _ _ _ _ _ is a group in a population who are of a different race or culture than the dominant one.
- E _ _ _ _ _ _ _ _ _ is when you painlessly end someone's life if they are in pain and are terminally ill.
- A n _ _ _ _ _ _ _ _ _ _ _ _ is a person who is different and does not follow the normal ways of thinking or behaving.
- E _ _ _ _ _ _ _ _ means having ideas that are very radical, such as political or religious ideas.
- A r _ _ _ is a violent protest about something, resulting in public disorder.
- An i _ _ _ _ _ _ _ _ _ _ _ is a person who is living in a country illegally.
- S _ _ _ _ _ h _ _ _ _ _ _ _ _ _ is when you bother or annoy someone for sexual reasons.
- A s _ _ _ _ _ _ - p _ _ _ _ _ f _ _ _ _ _ is a family that has only a mother or father.
- D _ _ _ a _ _ _ _ refers to the illegal use of drugs for recreational purposes.

114

Unit 12: Music and Arts

- A p _ _ _ _ _ _ _ _ _ _ is the presentation of a form of entertainment, such as a play.
- A s _ _ _ _ _ _ _ o _ _ _ _ _ _ is when people stand up and clap after an outstanding performance.
- An a _ _ _ _ _ _ _ _ _ is a person who knows a lot about, and is very interested in, a particular subject.
- A m _ _ _ _ _ _ is an afternoon performance of a play, film, etc.
- An a _ _ _ _ _ _ _ _ _ _ _ _ is a true story someone writes about the things that have happened in their life.
- A c _ _ _ _ _ _ _ is someone who writes music.
- A v _ _ _ _ is a place where an event or performance takes place.
- An o _ _ _ _ _ _ _ _ is a large group of people who play different classical musical instruments together.
- An e _ _ _ _ _ _ _ _ _ is a show or display of art.
- P _ _ _ _ _ is a type of writing where the sounds of the words are as important as their meanings.
- A _ _ _ _ _ _ _ _ relates to what is regarded as being beautiful.
- A f _ _ _ _ _ _ _ is a celebration involving a lot of people relating to a specific occasion.
- N _ _ f _ _ _ _ _ _ refers to stories that are factual and true.
- A m _ _ _ _ _ _ is a film or play containing lots of music, singing, and dancing.
- A _ _ _ a _ _ c _ _ _ _ _ refer to a hobby in which people make decorative items for the home.
- F _ _ _ _ _ _ refers to imaginary stories written for entertainment purposes.
- An a _ _ _ _ _ _ _ is the people who watch or listen to a performance, such as a play or a concert.
- A p _ _ _ _ _ _ _ is a person who plays the plays the piano.
- An o _ _ _ _ is a play with music, where actors sing instead of speaking.
- A m _ _ _ _ _ _ _ _ _ _ is an outstanding work of art.
- B _ _ _ _ _ is a type of classical dance involving dancing on the tips of your toes.
- An a _ _ g _ _ _ _ _ _ is a building where works of art are displayed and viewed.
- A p _ _ _ _ _ _ _ is a painting of a person.
- A s _ _ _ _ l _ _ _ is a painting of objects that does not include people or a landscape, such as a bowl of fruit.

Unit 13: Advertising

- To p _ _ _ is an informal word used for the act of promoting a product or service.
- A u _ _ _ _ _ s _ _ _ _ _ _ p _ _ _ _ (USP) is something that makes a product different from other products and therefore special.
- The t _ _ _ _ _ a _ _ _ _ _ _ _ is the type, class, or age of people a company is trying to sell its product to.
- An a _ _ _ _ _ _ _ _ _ c _ _ _ _ _ _ _ is a strategy designed to create a demand for a product or service.
- C _ _ _ - c _ _ _ _ _ _ is the practice of selling things by telephone to people who are called at random.
- P _ _ _ _ _ _ _ a _ _ are advertisements used by people to find new friends, partners, or companions.
- S _ _ _ _ _ _ _ _ _ _ is when a company/organisation gives money to a sports team or event in return for publicity.
- E _ _ - c _ _ _ _ _ _ _ _ means very noticeable because it is very prominent or different.
- A j _ _ _ _ _ is a short tune accompanying an advertisement on television, radio, or the internet.
- A l _ _ _ is an image or design closely associated with a company or product, used for marketing purposes.
- A b _ _ _ _ _ _ _ _ is a large roadside sign visible from some distance away that advertises a product or service.
- A c _ _ _ _ _ _ _ _ e _ _ _ _ _ _ _ _ _ _ is when a well-known person promotes a particular product or service.
- C _ _ _ _ _ _ _ _ _ a _ _ are small advertisements placed in a newspaper or online by the general public to sell items that they no longer want or need.
- A p _ _ _ _ _ _ l _ _ _ _ _ is when a company introduces a new product onto the market.
- A b _ _ _ _ is a name associated with a specific product or range of products made by a particular company.
- A s _ _ _ _ _ is a short, catchy phrase used to sell a product.
- H _ _ _ refers to exaggerated claims about the value of a product or service to make it sound better than it really is.
- P _ _ _ _ _ _ p _ _ _ _ _ _ _ _ is when a product is seen or used in a television programme or film for advertising purposes.
- A c _ _ _ _ _ _ _ _ _ is an advertisement on radio or television.
- A s _ _ _ _ _ _ o _ _ _ _ is a discounted price or special deal used to get people to buy a product or service.
- B _ _ _ _ l _ _ _ _ _ _ is when customers only purchase a particular brand.
- T _ _ _ _ _ _ _ _ refers to selling products and services over the phone.
- An a _ _ _ _ _ _ _ _ _ _ a _ _ _ _ _ is a company that specialises in promoting the products and services of others.
- S _ _ _ _ _ _ _ _ _ a _ _ _ _ _ _ _ _ _ _ is advertising delivered in such a way that people are unaware of it as it works on an unconscious level.

116

Unit 14: Education

- A s _ _ _ _ _ _ _ _ _ _ is a financial award from an organisation, individual, or government that helps a student pay for their education.
- A s _ _ _ _ _ _ (BE) is a small study group of students and their tutor at university.
- A l _ _ _ _ _ _ is a formal talk/lesson on a specific subject at university.
- A f _ _ _ _ _ _ (BE) is a department at a university that is based on an area of study, like law or history.
- A t _ _ _ _ _ _ _ (BE) is similar to a seminar but with fewer students or just one student.
- A d _ _ _ _ _ is an award/qualification that you get when you have successfully finished university.
- A s _ _ _ _ _ _ _ is the list of topics that you study on a specific course.
- T _ _ _ _ _ _ _ _ _ _ refers to the special technical or scientific words related to a particular area of study/work.
- An u _ _ _ _ _ _ _ _ _ _ _ _ is a student at university who is studying for their first degree.
- A p _ _ _ _ _ _ _ _ _ _ is a student at university who is studying for a higher degree.
- A d _ _ _ _ _ _ _ _ _ _ _ / t _ _ _ _ _ is a long, formal piece of written work at university containing original research and normally required in order to receive a Master's degree or Ph.D.
- An a _ _ _ _ _ _ _ _ _ is a piece of homework at school or university.
- A P _ . _ . is the highest qualification you can get at university; the abbreviation for 'Doctor of Philosophy'.
- A M _ _ _ _ _ _ ` _ d _ _ _ _ _ is a higher degree you can study for after a first degree.
- A p _ _ _ _ is a student at primary or secondary school.
- A s _ _ _ _ s _ _ _ _ _ is a school that provides a free education and is funded by the government.
- D _ _ _ _ _ _ _ _ l _ _ _ _ _ _ _ _ is learning online/at home without having to attend the university or college which awards the qualification.
- To g _ _ _ _ _ _ _ _ is to obtain a qualification – especially a degree at university.
- A c _ _ _ _ _ _ _ _ _ _ refers to the subjects offered by a school or college that can be studied there.
- L _ _ _ _ _ _ _ _ is the ability to read and write.
- To be i _ _ _ _ _ _ _ _ is not to know how to read or write.
- P _ _ _ _ _ _ e _ _ _ _ _ _ _ _ _ is education from about the ages of about five to 11; elementary education.
- S _ _ _ _ _ _ _ _ _ e _ _ _ _ _ _ _ _ is education from the ages of about 11 to 18.
- T _ _ _ _ _ _ _ e _ _ _ _ _ _ _ _ _ refers to higher education – normally at university.

Unit 15: Crime

- A l _ _ _ _ _ is a person who works in and knows about the law.
- To be i _ _ _ _ _ _ _ is not to be responsible for a crime.
- An a _ _ _ _ is a reason or evidence that proves you could not have committed a crime.
- A c _ _ _ _ _ _ is a person who broke the law or did something wrong.
- A j _ _ _ is a group of ordinary people in court who are presented with the facts of a case and decide whether a person is innocent or guilty.
- A j _ _ _ _ is the person who is in charge in a courtroom.
- A b _ _ _ _ _ _ _ _ (BE) is a lawyer who defends people in court.
- A c _ _ _ _ is a place where it is decided if someone is innocent or guilty.
- A t _ _ _ _ is a process to decide if someone is innocent or guilty.
- A v _ _ _ _ _ _ is a decision made by a judge or jury regarding someone's innocence or guilt.
- A v _ _ _ _ _ is someone who has suffered from a crime.
- To a _ _ _ _ _ is to formally challenge a decision, especially a verdict, in an attempt to get it changed.
- To b _ _ something is to not allow or forbid it.
- A s _ _ _ _ _ _ _ is a decision by a judge regarding the punishment after someone has been found guilty of a crime.
- C _ _ _ _ _ _ p _ _ _ _ _ _ _ _ is punishment by death for a serious crime.
- If something is a _ _ _ _ _ _ t _ _ l _ , it is illegal.
- You g _ _ a _ _ _ w _ _ s _ _ _ _ _ _ _ _ if you commit a crime and are not caught or are found innocent, even though you are guilty.
- A w _ _ _ _ _ is an object, such as a gun or knife, used to hurt or kill someone.
- To e _ _ _ _ _ is to get away from someone or something.
- To a _ _ _ _ _ s _ _ _ _ _ _ is when the police take someone to a police station on the suspicion of having committed a crime.
- To c _ _ _ _ _ a c _ _ _ _ is to do something wrong/break the law.
- C _ _ _ _ _ _ _ _ s _ _ _ _ _ _ is a punishment which involves helping in the community.
- A s _ _ _ _ _ _ _ _ (BE) is a person qualified to give legal advice.
- A d _ _ _ _ _ _ _ _ is the person in court accused of committing a crime.

118

Unit 16: Environment

- B _ _ _ _ _ _ _ _ _ _ _ refers to the number and variety of living things in a particular place.
- A c _ _ _ _ _ _ _ _ _ _ is a disaster.
- C _ _ _ _ _ _ refers to the regular weather conditions that occur in a particular area.
- To c _ _ _ _ _ _ _ _ _ _ means to pollute or make impure.
- To d _ _ o _ _ means to become extinct.
- An e _ _ _ _ _ _ _ _ is all the living and non-living things in a particular place and their interactions with each other.
- To be e _ _ _ _ _ _ _ _ _ means to be in danger of becoming extinct.
- E _ _ _ _ _ _ f _ _ _ _ are the polluting gases coming from an engine (for example, a car).
- To r _ _ _ _ _ _ is to convert waste, such as paper, glass, and plastic, into something that can be used again.
- To be g _ _ _ _ means to be friendly toward the environment.
- M _ _ _ _ _ l _ _ _ refers to the things that live in the sea.
- F _ _ _ _ _ f _ _ _ _ are sources of energy, such as coal and oil, formed from the remains of plants and animals which have been dead for a long time.
- F _ _ _ _ _ _ _ is a controversial way of extracting fossil fuels from rock.
- A t _ _ _ _ _ is a danger.
- R _ _ _ _ _ _ _ _ e _ _ _ _ _ is natural energy from the sun, wind, etc. that will always be available.
- To c _ _ _ _ _ _ _ something is to protect it so that it does not die out.
- A d _ _ _ _ _ _ is a long period without rain/water.
- S _ _ _ _ _ refers to waste products carried in water.
- To become e _ _ _ _ _ _ means to die out or cease to exist.
- The g _ _ _ _ _ _ _ _ _ _ e _ _ _ _ _ is what happens when gases get trapped in the atmosphere, warming up the earth.
- The o _ _ _ _ l _ _ _ _ is a layer in the stratosphere protecting life from the sun's radiation.
- G _ _ _ _ _ w _ _ _ _ _ _ refers to an increase in temperatures caused by increases in carbon dioxide and methane.
- C _ _ _ _ _ _ c _ _ _ _ _ refers to the changes in the climate – currently used to refer to those changes caused by human activity.
- S _ _ _ is a fog or haze caused by air pollution.

Unit 17: Geography

- A p _ _ _ _ _ _ _ _ is a thin strip of land surrounded on three sides by water.
- A c _ _ _ _ _ _ _ _ _ _ is an area with a lot of towns/cities close together.
- An e _ _ _ _ _ _ _ / the m _ _ _ _ is the wide part of a river where it flows into the sea.
- A p _ _ _ / s _ _ _ _ _ is the top of a mountain.
- An i _ _ _ _ _ _ is a gigantic piece of ice floating in the ocean or sea.
- A c _ _ _ _ _ _ is a deep valley made of rock that was carved out by a river over time.
- A g _ _ _ _ _ _ is a large, slowly moving river of ice.
- A r _ _ _ _ _ _ _ _ is a natural or artificial lake that supplies water for domestic consumption or use in industry.
- A b _ _ _ _ _ _ is an extremely large rock.
- A _ _ _ _ _ _ _ refers to how high something is above sea-level.
- The A _ _ _ _ _ is the area around the North Pole.
- The A _ _ _ _ _ _ _ _ is the area around the South Pole.
- A c _ _ _ _ _ _ _ _ _ _ _ is a person who makes maps.
- A c _ _ _ _ _ _ _ _ is one of the main landmasses on the earth, such as Asia, Europe, and Africa.
- A h _ _ _ _ _ _ _ _ _ is one of the two halves of the earth divided by the equator, separating them into northern and southern.
- L _ _ _ _ _ _ _ refers to how far a place is north or south of the equator, measured in degrees.
- L _ _ _ _ _ _ _ _ refers to how far a place is east or west of Greenwich, London, U.K., measured in degrees.
- A m _ _ _ _ _ _ _ _ r _ _ _ _ is a line of mountains that are more or less connected together.
- H _ _ _ _ refers to an area with lots of small, rounded mountains.
- R _ _ _ _ _ refers to ground having an uneven and rocky terrain.
- A m _ _ _ _ is a very small hill.
- A c _ _ _ _ is a hill with a flat, vertical surface, usually located near the edge of the sea.
- A g _ _ _ _ is a narrow, steep-sided valley.
- A b _ _ _ _ is a very small river.

Unit 18: Health and Medicine

- An a _ _ _ _ _ _ _ _ is when a part of the body is removed (e.g., an arm or a leg) in a medical procedure.
- F _ _ _ _ means resulting in death.
- The i _ _ _ _ _ s _ _ _ _ _ is the parts of the body that fight diseases and viruses.
- A _ _ _ _ means quick to become serious or severe, but lasting only a short time.
- C _ _ _ _ _ _ means lasting a long time.
- When you are d _ _ _ _ _ _ _ _ _, you don't have enough water in your body.
- B _ _ _ _ _ means not harmful.
- F _ _ _ _ a _ _ is the initial treatment people receive when they suffer an injury.
- A h _ _ _ _ _ _ _ _ _ _ _ is a person who always imagine they are ill, even when they are not.
- R _ _ _ _ _ _ _ _ _ _ is a treatment for cancer using high-energy x-rays.
- A d _ _ _ _ _ _ _ _ is a medical explanation of an illness.
- D _ _ _ _ _ _ _ is when someone suffers from a loss of mental faculties, such as memory; it usually affects older people.
- A g _ _ _ is a microorganism that causes disease or sickness.
- To t _ _ _ _ _ _ _ _ _ means to take an organ, for example a kidney, from one person and put it in someone else's body.
- M _ _ _ _ _ _ _ _ refers to something that is expected to grow and get worse, probably resulting in death.
- The s _ _ _ - e _ _ _ _ _ _ are the unwanted, bad effects of taking a medicine.
- A p _ _ _ _ _ _ _ _ _ _ _ is a written piece of paper that indicates the correct type and amount of medicine that you need and how often you should take it, according to a doctor.
- If you are p _ _ _ _ _ _ _ _, you are unable to move or feel all or a part of your body.
- A v _ _ _ _ is a dangerous, microscopic organism that causes the spread of diseases.
- A w _ _ _ _ is an injury to a body, especially to the skin.
- A s _ _ _ _ _ _ is a doctor who specialises in performing operations.
- A _ _ _ _ _ _ _ is a loss of memory.
- A s _ _ _ _ _ _ is the outward sign of an illness.
- C _ _ _ _ _ _ _ _ _ _ _ is a type of treatment for cancer using chemicals that are injected into the body.

Unit 19: Science and Technology

- A g _ _ _ _ _ is a small device/invention, usually novel and ingenious.
- To m _ _ _ p _ _ _ _ _ _ _ is to make something better or to get closer to completing something.
- N _ _ _ _ _ _ _ _ _ _ _ _ is the science/technology of working with very small things.
- A g _ _ _ / n _ _ _ is a person obsessed with technology who some people consider to be boring and socially inept.
- S _ _ _ _ - o _ - t _ _ - a _ _ refers to the latest/newest model/technology.
- O _ _ _ _ _ _ _ refers to technology that is no longer new or in fashion.
- To d _ _ _ _ _ _ _ _ _ something is to show how something is done.
- An e _ _ _ _ _ _ _ _ _ is a scientific procedure undertaken to discover something new.
- I _ _ _ _ _ _ _ _ _ refers to the introduction of new things or methods.
- H _ _ _ - t _ _ _ refers to something that uses or requires the latest technology.
- To c _ _ _ _ _ _ _ things is to arrange them according to their type/category.
- To be c _ _ _ _ _ _ _ _ - l _ _ _ _ _ _ _ is to know how to use computers.
- A m _ _ _ _ _ _ _ _ is a very small but important part of many electronic devices.
- To d _ _ _ _ _ _ something is to make it more advanced/better.
- 'C _ _ _ _ -' is a prefix denoting that something is related to computers or the internet.
- C _ _ _ _ _ _ _ e _ _ _ refers to the very latest technology, research, design, etc.
- If something is o _ _ _ _ _ _ _ _ , it is out-of-date and no longer in use.
- A l _ _ _ _ _ _ - s _ _ _ _ _ device is one which reduces the amount of work or effort needed.
- To r _ _ _ _ _ _ _ is to investigate and study something to find out new things.
- A t _ _ _ _ _ _ _ _ _ _ is a person who is afraid of technology.
- A b _ _ _ _ _ _ _ _ _ _ is a sudden and important discovery.
- A h _ _ _ _ _ _ _ _ _ / t _ _ _ _ _ is an idea that needs to be tested to see if it is true.
- I _ _ _ _ _ _ _ _ _ _ _ _ t _ _ _ _ _ _ _ _ _ (IT) refers to the study and use of computers or other electronic equipment to send/store information.
- A s _ _ _ _ _ e _ _ _ _ _ is a programme that helps you find information on the internet.

Unit 20: Work

- An e _ _ _ _ _ _ _ is someone who works for someone else.
- An e _ _ _ _ _ _ is someone who/a company that has other people that work him/her/ it.
- To r _ _ _ _ _ / q _ _ _ is to tell your employer that you no longer want to work for them.
- To be m _ _ _ r _ _ _ _ _ _ _ _ (BE) is to lose your job because you are no longer needed by your employer; to be laid off.
- O _ _ _ _ _ _ _ is time worked in addition to your normal hours.
- F _ _ _ _ _ _ _ _ is a system where you do not have fixed start and finish times when working, but start and finish when you want, while still working the same total number of hours per week/month.
- To be s _ _ _ _ _ / f _ _ _ _ is to lose your job because you've done something wrong.
- A p _ _ _ _ _ _ _ _ _ is an occupation that requires training and formal qualifications.
- To be u _ _ _ _ _ _ _ _ _ is to be without a job when you are in need of one.
- A t _ _ _ _ _ _ is a person learning to do a job.
- A w _ _ _ is the amount of money you earn (normally per hour or per week).
- Your o _ _ _ _ _ _ _ _ is the type of job you have.
- A c _ _ _ _ _ _ _ _ _ v _ _ _ _ (CV) is information about your education, past employment, etc. used when applying for a job.
- To do s _ _ _ _ - w _ _ _ is to work irregular hours (different hours on different days).
- A s _ _ _ _ _ is the amount of money you earn (normally per year).
- To have a f _ _ _ t _ _ _ j _ _ is to work about 40 hours per week.
- An i _ _ _ _ _ is a young person who is working somewhere to get experience and is not getting paid for that work.
- An a _ _ _ _ _ _ _ _ _ is a person learning how to do a job from someone who is skilled at doing it.
- Q _ _ _ _ _ _ _ _ _ _ _ _ _ are the education or the experience you have that make you suitable for a particular job.
- M _ _ _ _ _ _ _ _ l _ _ _ _ is the time off work given to women who have just had a baby.
- The C _ _ _ _ E _ _ _ _ _ _ _ _ O _ _ _ _ _ _ (CEO) is the person with the most important job in a company.
- To h _ _ _ i _ y _ _ _ n _ _ _ _ _ is to tell your employer you no longer want to work for them.
- U _ _ _ _ _ _ _ _ _ _ _ b _ _ _ _ _ _ is the money you get from the government if you are not working.
- To g _ o _ s _ _ _ _ _ is to stop working as a protest about something you don't like about your job or your employer.

Useful Collocations

Match the collocations in A with the definitions in B.

A	B
(1) to become widespread	(a) to change a great deal
(2) environmental degradation	(b) to have a bad effect on something
(3) to adversely affect	(c) the destruction of the environment
(4) to vary considerably	(d) to become common over a wide area

A	B
(1) preferential treatment	(a) a situation where everyone has the same opportunities to do something
(2) equal opportunities	(b) when a subject causes disagreements and arguments
(3) highly controversial	(c) a big problem
(4) a major challenge	(d) when a person is given special treatment and privileges

A	B
(1) markedly different	(a) to be treated worse than other people are for no good reason
(2) a rapid expansion	(b) a sudden increase
(3) to seem plausible	(c) very different
(4) to face discrimination	(d) to appear to be possible

A	B
(1) foreign investment	(a) to know new things
(2) unintended consequences	(b) almost everyone or everything
(3) the vast majority	(c) the effects of doing something that you didn't expect to happen
(4) to acquire knowledge	(d) the money invested in a country by other countries

A	B
(1) pioneering work	(a) when someone is given money to help them pay for something
(2) financial assistance	(b) quite new
(3) relatively recent	(c) much better than before
(4) a significant improvement	(d) groundbreaking work that paves the way for future developments

A	B
(1) a causal link	(a) to continue learning throughout your life
(2) lifelong learning	(b) believed to be true by everyone everywhere
(3) universally accepted	(c) just coming into existence now
(4) newly emerging	(d) when one thing causes something else to happen

Complete the gaps in the sentences below using the collocations above. You might have to change the form of the words so that they fit into the sentence grammatically.

1. The government is trying to promote _____ _____. They believe that people should continue studying when they leave school.
2. Mastering a foreign language can be a _____ _____. It requires hard work and dedication.
3. Staying up late the night before an exam can _____ _____ you performance in it. It is a much better idea to get a good night's sleep so that you are fresh in the morning and can perform well in the exam.
4. It has been shown that there is a _____ _____ between smoking and lung cancer.
5. It is widely accepted that men and women should have _____ _____ and that there should be no discrimination in the employment market.
6. Income distribution throughout the world _____ _____. In some countries there is a wide gap between the rich and the poor.
7. It is hard to believe that the internet is a _____ _____ development. It was not widespread until the turn of the last century.
8. The _____ _____ of people these days own a mobile phone. There are not many people who don't have one.
9. The landscape in the Netherlands, where it is very flat, is _____ _____ from the landscape in Switzerland, where it is very mountainous.
10. Some things have _____ _____. In the past, people did not realise how pollution would affect the environment.
11. The purpose of education should not just be to _____ _____, but also to enable people to think critically.
12. _____ _____ have been made to mobile phones in recent years. The phones of today are almost unrecognisable from those of forty years ago, which were very simple.

126

Useful Idioms

Match the idioms in A with the definitions in B.

A	B
(1) a no brainer	(a) It is what you do that matters, not what you say
(2) a hot potato	(b) a situation where the choice between different things is obvious
(3) to see eye to eye	(c) to agree with somebody about something
(4) actions speak louder than words	(d) a controversial topic

A	B
(1) when pigs fly	(a) this is used to say that something is very unlikely to happen
(2) to be over the moon	(b) to attempt to do more than you are capable of doing
(3) the best thing since sliced bread	(c) to be very happy
(4) to bite off more than you can chew	(d) to be very good

A	B
(1) to miss the boat	(a) you shouldn't judge somebody or something solely by outward appearances
(2) shouldn't judge a book by its cover	(b) to disclose a secret
(3) to cry over spilt milk	(c) to be upset about something that you can't change
(4) to let the cat out of the bag	(d) to miss the opportunity to do something because you are too late

A	B
(1) wouldn't be caught dead	(a) to eventually tell somebody something that they really want to know
(2) to spill the beans	(b) this is used to say that you won't do something under any circumstances at all
(3) to give someone the cold shoulder	(c) to not feel very well
(4) to feel a bit under the weather	(d) to ignore somebody

A	B
(1) to give somebody the benefit of the doubt	(a) to come up with the exactly correct answer or solution to a problem
(2) to hit the nail on the head	(b) to say something using just a few words
(3) to be on the ball	(c) to believe somebody even though there is no evidence that they are being truthful
(4) to cut a long story short	(d) to know exactly what is happening

A	B
(1) to cost an arm and a leg	(a) not very often
(2) to be a pain in the neck	(b) to be irritating or annoying
(3) be a piece of cake	(c) to be very expensive
(4) once in a blue moon	(d) to be very easy

Complete the sentences below with the idioms above. You may have to change the form of the words so that they fit into the sentence grammatically.

13. I _____ _____ _____ _____ wearing a shirt like that. It looks ridiculous!

14. The exam was a _____ _____ _____. I couldn't believe how easy it was.

15. She normally cooks for herself and only eats out at restaurants _____ _____ _____ _____ _____.

16. My grandfather is nearly ninety, but he is really _____ _____ _____. He understands everything that is going on in the world.

17. My sister's smart phone _____ _____ _____ _____ _____ _____. I think it's a complete waste of money.

18. It's no use _____ _____ _____ _____. There is nothing you can do about it now, so stop worrying about it.

19. I didn't go to school yesterday as I was _____ _____ _____ _____ _____ _____. I feel much better today, though.

20. It's too late to register for the course. You've _____ _____ _____, I'm afraid.

21. That's the perfect solution! You've _____ _____ _____ _____ _____ _____.

22. I think you've _____ _____ _____ _____ _____ _____ _____. There is no way you will be able to do that before the end of the month.

23. My brother's a _____ _____ _____ _____. He's always disturbing me when I'm trying to do my homework.

24. We don't always _____ _____ _____ _____, but on this occasion we were in complete agreement.

Useful Vocabulary for the Essay

Match the words in A with the definitions in B.

A	B
(1) exacerbate(v.)	(a) something that people believe that is not true
(2) inconceivable (adj.)	(b) possible
(3) feasible (adj.)	(c) not possible
(4) (a) misconception (n.)	(d) to make worse

A	B
(1) (the) optimum (n.)	(a) current, relating to society today
(2) detrimental (adj.)	(b) impossible to prevent from happening
(3) unavoidable (adj.)	(c) the best possible
(4) contemporary (adj.)	(d) harmful

A	B
(1) indispensable (adj.)	(a) absolutely necessary
(2) attainable (adj.)	(b) never having happened before
(3) ascertain (v.)	(c) to find out
(4) unparalleled (adj.)	(d) possible to get or achieve in the future

A	B
(1) principal (adj.)	(a) very important
(2) vulnerable (adj.)	(b) main
(3) unprecedented (adj.)	(c) easily harmed or damaged
(4) vital (adj.)	(d) never having happened before

A	B
(1) crucial (adj.)	(a) possible
(2) viable (adj.)	(b) much better than or very different from what is considered to be normal
(3) exceptional (adj.)	(c) certain to happen
(4) inevitable (adj.)	(d) very important

A	B
(1) deteriorate (v.)	(a) to be able to continue into the future
(2) beneficial (adj.)	(b) believable
(3) credible (adj.)	(c) to get worse
(4) sustainable (adj.)	(d) to have positive effects

Complete the sentences below with the words above. You may have to change the form of some of the words so that they fit into the sentence grammatically. More than one word may fit.

1. Some research suggests that the _____ number of students in an English class is eight. Students in classes of this size get the best results.
2. All food, with the exception of honey, _____ over time. Honey, on the other hand, never goes bad.
3. It is _____ that you get a good night's sleep before the IELTS exam. If you do, you will be fresh and perform better in the exam.
4. To get a band nine in the IELTs exam is _____. It is possible, however.
5. Advertising should not be directed at young people as they are particularly

    _____.
6. Using fossil fuels has a _____ effect on the environment. They pollute the atmosphere and cause global warming.
7. The use of renewable energy, such as solar and wind power, on the other hand, would have a _____ effect on the environment.
8. Furthermore, the use of fossil fuels is not _____, as the supply of oil and coal will eventually be exhausted.
9. Forest fires are a problem in some parts of the world. A strong wind will fan the flames of the fire and _____ the situation.
10. No matter how careful you are, some accidents are _____. They just can't be prevented.
11. The _____ ingredient of steak tartare is raw beef.
12. It was decided that the proposed new airport was not _____, as it would cost too much to build.

Answer Key

Unit 1: Globalisation

Matching

1.	c	1.	c	1.	d	1.	d	1.	c	1.	b
2.	b	2.	d	2.	a	2.	c	2.	a	2.	a
3.	a	3.	b	3.	c	3.	b	3.	b	3.	c
4.	d	4.	a	4.	b	4.	a	4.	d	4.	d

Complete the Sentences

1. superpower
2. franchises
3. emigration
4. multinational corporation
5. stocks and shares
6. exports
7. standard of living
8. recession
9. outsource
10. consumption
11. economic growth
12. imports

Unit 2: Money and Finance

Matching

1.	d	1.	c	1.	d	1.	b	1.	d	1.	c
2.	c	2.	a	2.	a	2.	c	2.	b	2.	d
3.	a	3.	b	3.	b	3.	d	3.	a	3.	a
4.	b	4.	d	4.	c	4.	a	4.	c	4.	b

Complete the Sentences

1. cost of living
2. income tax
3. exchange rate
4. mortgage
5. worthless
6. rebate
7. fees
8. pension
9. black market
10. debit card
11. credit card
12. priceless

Unit 3: Food

Matching

1.	d	1.	a	1.	c	1.	d	1.	c	1.	a
2.	c	2.	b	2.	a	2.	c	2.	b	2.	b
3.	a	3.	c	3.	d	3.	b	3.	d	3.	c
4.	b	4.	d	4.	b	4.	a	4.	c	4.	d

Complete the Sentences

1. vegetarian
2. obesity
3. healthy appetite
4. balanced diet
5. food poisoning
6. snacks
7. malnourished
8. fast food
9. portions
10. canteen/refractory
11. overweight or obese
12. vitamin

Unit 4: Sport and Leisure

Matching

1.	c	1.	b	1.	d	1.	d	1.	b	1.	c
2.	d	2.	d	2.	a	2.	c	2.	a	2.	b
3.	a	3.	a	3.	b	3.	b	3.	d	3.	a
4.	b	4.	c	4.	c	4.	a	4.	c	4.	d

Complete the Sentences

1. have a picnic
2. couch potato
3. take a stroll
4. trekking
5. social life
6. stadium
7. sedentary
8. let off steam
9. spectators
10. Jacuzzi
11. referee
12. squad

Stop and Check: Units 1–4

Globalisation

1. affluence
2. consumption
3. multinational corporation
4. emigration
5. immigrate
6. recession
7. export
8. stocks and shares

Money and Finance

1. credit card
2. on credit
3. interest
4. bankrupt
5. pension
6. well off
7. expenditure
8. the cost of living

Food

1. balanced diet
2. fast food
3. portion
4. protein
5. confectionery
6. obesity
7. food poisoning
8. allergy

Sport and Leisure

1. trekking
2. sedentary
3. couch potato
4. bungee jumping
5. have a picnic
6. take a stroll
7. stadium
8. work-life balance

Unit 5: Politics

Matching

1.	a	1.	b	1.	d	1.	c	1.	b	1.	d
2.	d	2.	a	2.	c	2.	d	2.	d	2.	a
3.	b	3.	d	3.	b	3.	b	3.	c	3.	c
4.	c	4.	c	4.	a	4.	a	4.	a	4.	b

Complete the Sentences

1. candidate
2. election
3. political parties
4. coalition
5. prime minister
6. ideologies
7. monarchy
8. nationalistic/patriotic
9. referendum
10. socialist
11. coup
12. right-wing

Unit 6: Travel and Transport

Matching

1.	b	1.	b	1.	c	1.	b	1.	b	1.	c
2.	c	2.	a	2.	d	2.	c	2.	a	2.	d
3.	d	3.	d	3.	a	3.	d	3.	d	3.	a
4.	a	4.	c	4.	b	4.	a	4.	c	4.	b

Complete the Sentences

1. long-haul
2. detour
3. hand luggage
4. ferry
5. canal
6. cab
7. facilities
8. jet lag
9. aviation
10. check-in
11. immigration
12. ecotourism

Unit 7: Media

Matching

1.	a	1.	d	1.	d	1.	b	1.	d	1.	d
2.	d	2.	a	2.	b	2.	c	2.	a	2.	c
3.	b	3.	c	3.	a	3.	a	3.	b	3.	a
4.	c	4.	b	4.	c	4.	d	4.	c	4.	b

Complete the Sentences

1. paparazzi
2. live
3. well-informed
4. documentary
5. satellite
6. editor
7. current affairs
8. censorship
9. free press
10. horoscope
11. proprietor
12. headline

Unit 8: Architecture

Matching

1.	b	1.	c	1.	d	1.	b	1.	b	1.	a
2.	c	2.	d	2.	a	2.	a	2.	c	2.	c
3.	d	3.	a	3.	c	3.	d	3.	d	3.	d
4.	a	4.	b	4.	b	4.	c	4.	a	4.	b

Complete the Sentences

1. cottage
2. civil engineer
3. derelict
4. eyesore
5. insulation
6. demolished
7. slum
8. storey (BE)/story (AE)
9. construction
10. gated community
11. skyscrapers
12. detached house

Stop and Check: Units 5–8

Politics

1. ideology
2. vote
3. political party
4. radical
5. conservative
6. referendum
7. totalitarian
8. coup

Travel and Transport

1. terminal
2. check-in
3. immigration
4. hand luggage
5. long-haul
6. jet lag
7. cab
8. facilities

Media

1. free press
2. censorship
3. proprietor
4. current affairs
5. soap opera
6. documentary
7. live
8. pay-per-view

Architecture

1. detached house
2. bedsit/studio apartment
3. low-rise
4. high-rise
5. skyscraper
6. cottage
7. slum
8. well-designed

Unit 9: Town and Country

Matching

1.	d	1.	b	1.	c	1.	b	1.	c	1.	b
2.	c	2.	a	2.	a	2.	c	2.	d	2.	a
3.	b	3.	d	3.	d	3.	a	3.	a	3.	d
4.	a	4.	c	4.	b	4.	d	4.	b	4.	c

Complete the Sentences

1.   cosmopolitan
2.   urban sprawl
3.   megacities
4.   irrigation
5.   depopulation
6.   outskirts
7.   the rush hour
8.   traffic congestion
9.   rural
10.   urban
11.   public transport
12.   pedestrian precinct

Unit 10: Family

Matching

1.	d	1.	b	1.	c	1.	b	1.	c	1.	c
2.	c	2.	a	2.	d	2.	c	2.	a	2.	d
3.	a	3.	d	3.	a	3.	a	3.	d	3.	b
4.	b	4.	c	4.	b	4.	d	4.	b	4.	a

Complete the Sentences

1. arranged marriages
2. juvenile
3. ancestors
4. sibling
5. breadwinner
6. divorce
7. adoption
8. extended family
9. elderly
10. senior citizens
11. stepmother
12. guardian

Unit 11: Social Issues

Matching

1.	b	1.	d	1.	c	1.	b	1.	a	1.	b
2.	c	2.	a	2.	d	2.	c	2.	c	2.	a
3.	d	3.	b	3.	a	3.	d	3.	d	3.	d
4.	a	4.	c	4.	b	4.	a	4.	b	4.	c

Complete the Sentences

1. refugee
2. single-parent families
3. drug abuse
4. political asylum
5. civil rights
6. terrorism
7. ethnic minority
8. riots
9. discrimination
10. animal rights
11. outcasts
12. euthanasia

Unit 12: Music and Arts

Matching

1.	d	1.	c	1.	b	1.	a	1.	d	1.	b
2.	a	2.	d	2.	c	2.	c	2.	c	2.	d
3.	b	3.	a	3.	d	3.	d	3.	a	3.	a
4.	c	4.	b	4.	a	4.	b	4.	b	4.	c

Complete the Sentences

1.   art gallery
2.   audience
3.   non-fiction
4.   masterpiece
5.   composer
6.   fiction
7.   aficionado
8.   matinee
9.   still life
10.   venue
11.   standing ovation
12.   autobiography

Stop and Check: Units 9–12

Town and Country

1. urban
2. rural
3. depopulation
4. overcrowding
5. traffic congestion
6. megacity
7. cosmopolitan
8. urban sprawl

Family

1. nuclear family
2. extended family
3. arranged marriage
4. siblings
5. divorce
6. the elderly
7. relatives
8. widow/widower

Social Issues

1. racism
2. dissident
3. ethnic minority
4. outcast
5. euthanasia
6. drug abuse
7. terrorism
8. ethnic cleansing/genocide

Music and the Arts

1. fiction
2. non-fiction
3. autobiography
4. art gallery
5. masterpiece
6. portrait
7. still life
8. aficionado

Unit 13: Advertising

Matching

1.	d	1.	c	1.	d	1.	b	1.	c	1.	c
2.	c	2.	d	2.	b	2.	a	2.	d	2.	d
3.	a	3.	b	3.	a	3.	d	3.	a	3.	a
4.	b	4.	a	4.	c	4.	c	4.	b	4.	b

Complete the Sentences

1. personal ad
2. sponsorship
3. hype
4. special offer
5. unique selling point
6. billboard
7. advertising agency
8. target audience
9. classified ads
10. brand loyalty
11. advertising campaign
12. commercial

Unit 14: Education

Matching

1.	c	1.	a	1.	c	1.	b	1.	d	1.	d
2.	a	2.	d	2.	d	2.	a	2.	c	2.	a
3.	d	3.	b	3.	b	3.	d	3.	a	3.	b
4.	b	4.	c	4.	a	4.	c	4.	b	4.	c

Complete the Sentences

1.   pupil
2.   Ph.D.
3.   terminology
4.   distance learning
5.   dissertation/thesis
6.   state school
7.   illiterate
8.   assignments
9.   primary education
10.   syllabus
11.   curriculum
12.   lecture

Unit 15: Crime

Matching

1.	c	1.	d	1.	d	1.	d	1.	b	1.	d
2.	a	2.	b	2.	a	2.	c	2.	c	2.	a
3.	d	3.	c	3.	b	3.	b	3.	a	3.	b
4.	b	4.	a	4.	c	4.	a	4.	d	4.	c

Complete the Sentences

1.   got away with
2.   judge
3.   trial
4.   alibi
5.   jury
6.   arrested
7.   community service
8.   to appeal
9.   weapon
10.   banned
11.   victim
12.   escaped

Unit 16: Environment

Matching

1.	b	1.	d	1.	c	1.	d	1.	b	1.	a
2.	a	2.	a	2.	b	2.	a	2.	c	2.	c
3.	d	3.	c	3.	a	3.	b	3.	a	3.	d
4.	c	4.	b	4.	d	4.	c	4.	d	4.	b

Complete the Sentences

1.   ozone layer
2.   dying out
3.   fossil fuels
4.   smog
5.   marine life
6.   exhaust fumes
7.   climate
8.   threat
9.   green
10.   sewage
11.   climate change
12.   recycle

Stop and Check: Units 13–16

Advertising

1. commercial
2. advertising agency
3. advertising campaign
4. brand
5. slogan
6. jingle
7. logo
8. classified ads

Education

1. primary education
2. literacy
3. secondary education
4. tertiary education
5. undergraduate
6. lecture
7. graduate
8. postgraduate

Crime

1. victim
2. weapon
3. trial
4. verdict
5. appeal
6. capital punishment
7. community service
8. get away with something

Environment

1. climate change
2. greenhouse effect
3. drought
4. sewage
5. marine life
6. fossil fuels
7. recycle
8. contaminate

Unit 17: Geography

Matching

1.	d	1.	a	1.	d	1.	d	1.	a	1.	d
2.	a	2.	d	2.	a	2.	c	2.	c	2.	a
3.	b	3.	c	3.	c	3.	a	3.	b	3.	b
4.	c	4.	b	4.	b	4.	b	4.	d	4.	c

Complete the Sentences

1. hemisphere, hemisphere
2. mountain range
3. latitude, longitude
4. Antarctic
5. hilly
6. altitude
7. iceberg
8. continents
9. summit/peak
10. reservoir
11. conurbations

Unit 18: Health and Medicine

Matching

1.	d	1.	d	1.	b	1.	d	1.	b	1.	c
2.	a	2.	a	2.	a	2.	c	2.	d	2.	d
3.	c	3.	b	3.	d	3.	b	3.	a	3.	a
4.	b	4.	c	4.	c	4.	a	4.	c	4.	b

Complete the Sentences

1.   side-effects
2.   prescription
3.   transplant
4.   paralysed
5.   dehydrated
6.   wound
7.   amnesia
8.   fatal
9.   symptoms
10.   dementia
11.   benign
12.   germs

Unit 19: Science and Technology

Matching

1.	b	1.	c	1.	c	1.	b	1.	a	1.	b
2.	a	2.	d	2.	d	2.	d	2.	c	2.	d
3.	c	3.	a	3.	b	3.	a	3.	d	3.	a
4.	d	4.	b	4.	a	4.	c	4.	b	4.	c

Complete the Sentences

1. labour-saving
2. technophobe
3. information technology
4. state-of-the-art
5. outdated
6. research
7. demonstrated
8. computer-literate
9. breakthrough
10. search engine
11. geek/nerd
12. obsolete

Unit 20: Work

Matching

1.	b	1.	c	1.	b	1.	a	1.	a	1.	d
2.	c	2.	d	2.	a	2.	b	2.	c	2.	c
3.	d	3.	b	3.	d	3.	d	3.	d	3.	a
4.	a	4.	a	4.	c	4.	c	4.	b	4.	b

Complete the Sentences

1.   salary
2.   shift-work
3.   unemployment benefit
4.   curriculum vitae
5.   occupation
6.   full time
7.   flexitime
8.   overtime
9.   intern
10.   made redundant
11.   on strike
12.   hand in my notice

Stop and Check: Units 17–20

Geography

1. mountain range
2. altitude
3. hilly
4. brook
5. estuary/mouth
6. cartographer
7. latitude
8. longitude

Health and Medicine

1. diagnosis
2. prescription
3. side-effects
4. surgeon
5. transplant
6. fatal
7. chronic
8. hypochondriac

Science and Technology

1. gadget
2. labour-saving
3. geek/nerd
4. state-of-the-art/cutting edge
5. outdated
6. computer-literate
7. high-tech
8. technophobe

Work

1. qualifications
2. employer
3. full time
4. resign/quit/hand in your notice
5. made redundant
6. sacked/fired
7. unemployed
8. unemployment benefit

Useful Collocations

Matching

1.	d	1.	d	1.	c	1.	d	1.	d	1.	d
2.	c	2.	a	2.	b	2.	c	2.	a	2.	a
3.	b	3.	b	3.	d	3.	b	3.	b	3.	b
4.	a	4.	c	4.	a	4.	a	4.	c	4.	c

Complete the Sentences

1. lifelong learning
2. major challenge
3. adversely affect
4. causal link
5. equal opportunities
6. varies considerably
7. relatively recent
8. vast majority
9. markedly different
10. unintended consequences
11. acquire knowledge
12. significant improvements

Useful Idioms

Matching

1.	b	1.	a	1.	d	1.	b	1.	c	1.	c
2.	d	2.	c	2.	a	2.	a	2.	a	2.	b
3.	c	3.	d	3.	c	3.	d	3.	d	3.	d
4.	a	4.	b	4.	b	4.	c	4.	b	4.	a

Complete the Sentences

1. wouldn't be caught dead
2. piece of cake
3. once in a blue moon
4. on the ball
5. cost an arm and a leg
6. crying over spilt milk
7. feeling a bit under the weather
8. missed the boat
9. hit the nail on the head
10. bitten off more than you can chew
11. pain in the neck
12. see eye to eye

Useful Vocabulary for the Essay

Matching

1.	d	1.	c	1.	a	1.	b	1.	d	1.	c
2.	c	2.	d	2.	d	2.	c	2.	a	2.	d
3.	b	3.	b	3.	c	3.	d	3.	b	3.	b
4.	a	4.	a	4.	b	4.	a	4.	c	4.	a

Sentence Completion

1.   optimum
2.   deteriorates
3.   crucial/vital
4.   exceptional
5.   vulnerable
6.   detrimental
7.   beneficial
8.   sustainable
9.   exacerbate
10. unavoidable/inevitable
11. principal
12. viable/feasible

Topic Vocabulary Index

Unit 1: Globalisation

accounting

affluence

consumption

economic growth

emigration

export

franchise

immigrate

import

inflation

manufacturing

marketing

multinational corporation

outsource

prosperity

recession

standard of living

stock market

stocks and shares

superpower

tariff

taxation

the Balance of Trade

trade barrier

Unit 2: Money and Finance

bank loan

bankrupt

black market

cash

credit card

credit crunch

currency

debit card

deposit

exchange rate

expenditure

fee

income tax

interest

invest

mortgage

on credit

overdraft

pension

priceless

rebate

the cost of living

well off

worthless

Unit 3: Food

allergy

balanced diet

beverage

calorie

canteen (BE)/refectory (BE)

carbohydrate

cholesterol

confectionery

fast food

fat

food poisoning

genetically modified foods

have a healthy appetite

malnourished

minerals

nutrients

obesity

organic

overweight

portion

protein

snack

vegetarian

vitamins

vegetarian

vitamins

Unit 4: Sport and Leisure

bungee jumping

couch potato

equestrian

gymnastics

have a picnic

Jacuzzi

let off steam

lifestyle

marathon

martial arts

paragliding

recreational

referee

running track

scuba diving

sedentary

social life

spectators

squad

stadium

take a stroll

tenpin bowling

trekking

work-life balance

Unit 5: Politics

anarchism
candidate
coalition
committee
conservative
coup
democracy
election
ideology
left-wing
ministry
monarchy
nationalism
patriotic
policy
political party
president
prime minister
radical
referendum
right-wing
socialist
totalitarian
vote

Unit 6: Travel and Transport

all-inclusive

aviation

budget accommodation

cab

canal

check-in

destination

detour

disembark

ecotourism

embark

excursion

facilities

ferry

hand luggage

immigration

itinerary

jet lag

journey

long-haul

luxury accommodation

short-haul

terminal

trip

Unit 7: Media

broadcast
censorship
current affairs
documentary
editor
episode
free press
headline
horoscope
journal
journalism
live event
paparazzi
pay-per-view
presenter
proprietor
publisher
reporter
satellite
soap opera
subscription
tabloid
the press
well-informed

Unit 8: Architecture

balcony

bedsit/studio apartment

civil engineer

column

concrete

construction

cottage

demolish

derelict

detached house

eyesore

futuristic

gated community

high-rise

insulation

low-rise

modernist

patio

skyscraper

slum

storey (BE) / story (AE)

structure

terrace

well-designed

Unit 9: Town and Country

balcony

bedsit/studio apartment

civil engineer

column

concrete

construction

cottage

demolish

derelict

detached house

eyesore

futuristic

gated community

high-rise

insulation

low-rise

modernist

patio

skyscraper

slum

storey/story

structure

terrace

well-designed

Unit 10: Family

adolescent

adoption

ancestors

arranged marriage

bachelor

breadwinner

divorce

engagement

extended family

genes

geriatric

guardian

juvenile

maternal

nuclear family

offspring

paternal

relatives

senior citizen

siblings

stepmother and stepfather

the elderly

upbringing

widow/widower

Unit 11: Social Issues

abortion
animal rights
civil rights
discrimination
dissident
drug abuse
ethnic cleansing
ethnic minority
euthanasia
extremism
genocide
homelessness
human rights
illegal alien
nonconformist
outcast
political asylum
racism
refugee
riot
sexual harassment
single-parent family
squatter
terrorism

Unit 12: Music and Arts

aesthetic

aficionado

art gallery

arts and crafts

audience

autobiography

ballet

composer

exhibition

festival

fiction

masterpiece

matinee

musical

non-fiction

opera

orchestra

performance

pianist

poetry

portrait

standing ovation

still life

venue

Unit 13: Advertising

advertising agency

advertising campaign

billboard

brand

brand loyalty

celebrity endorsement

classified ads

cold-calling

commercial

eye-catching

hype

jingle

logo

personal ads

plug

product launch

product placement

slogan

special offer

sponsorship

subliminal advertising

target audience

telesales

unique selling point (USP)

Unit 14: Education

assignment

curriculum

degree

dissertation/thesis

distance learning

faculty

graduate

illiterate

lecture

literacy

Master's degree

Ph.D.

postgraduate

primary education

pupil

scholarship

secondary education

seminar

state school

syllabus

terminology

tertiary education

tutorial

undergraduate

Unit 15: Crime

lawyer

innocent

alibi

culprit

jury

judge

barrister

court

trial

verdict

victim

appeal

ban

sentence

capital punishment

against the law

get away with something

weapon

escape from something/someone

arrest someone

commit a crime

community service

solicitor

defendant

Unit 16: Environment

biodiversity

catastrophe

climate

climate change

conserve

contaminate

die out

drought

ecosystem

endangered

exhaust fumes

extinct

fossil fuels

fracking

global warming

green

greenhouse effect

marine life

ozone layer

recycle

renewable energy

sewage

smog

threat

Unit 17: Geography

peninsula

conurbation

estuary/mouth

peak/summit

iceberg

canyon

glacier

reservoir

boulder

altitude

Arctic

Antarctic

cartographer

continent

hemisphere

latitude

longitude

mountain range

hilly

rugged

mound

cliff

gorge

brook

Unit 18: Health and Medicine

acute

amnesia

amputation

benign

chemotherapy

chronic

dehydrated

dementia

diagnosis

fatal

first aid

germ

hypochondriac

immune system

malignant

paralysed

prescription

radiotherapy

side-effects

surgeon

symptom

transplant

virus

wound

Unit 19: Science and Technology

breakthrough

classify

computer-literate

cutting-edge

cyber

demonstrate

develop

experiment

gadget

geek/nerd

high-tech

hypothesis/theory

information technology (IT)

innovation

labour-saving

make progress

microchip

nanotechnology

obsolete

outdated

research

search engine

state-of-the-art

technophobe

Unit 20: Work

apprentice
CEO (Chief Executive Officer)
CV (curriculum vitae)
employee
employer
flexitime
full-time job
go on strike
hand in your notice
intern
made redundant (BE)
maternity leave
occupation
overtime
profession
qualifications
resign/quit
sacked/fired
salary
shift-work
trainee
unemployed
unemployment benefit
wage

Master Index

A

abortion
accounting
acute
adolescent
adoption
advertising agency
advertising campaign
aesthetic
affluence
aficionado
against the law
alibi
allergy
all-inclusive
altitude
amnesia
amputation
anarchism
ancestors
animal rights
Antarctic
appeal
apprentice
arable land
Arctic
arranged marriage
arrest someone
art gallery
arts and crafts
assignment
audience
autobiography
aviation

B

bachelor
Balance of Trade
balanced diet
balcony
ballet
ban
bank loan
bankrupt
barrister (BE)
bedsit/studio apartment
beggars
benign
beverage
billboard
biodiversity
black market
boulder
brand
brand loyalty
breadwinner
breakthrough
broadcast
brook
budget accommodation
bungee jumping

C

cab
calorie
canal
candidate
canteen (BE) / refectory (BE)
canyon
capital punishment
carbohydrate
cartographer

cash

catastrophe

celebrity endorsement

censorship

CEO (Chief Executive Officer)

check-in

chemotherapy

cholesterol

chronic

civil engineer

civil rights

classified ads

classify

cliff

climate

climate change

coalition

cold-calling

column

commercial

commit a crime

committee

community service

composer

computer-literate

concrete

confectionery

conservative

conserve

construction

consumption

contaminate

continent

conurbation

cosmopolitan

cost of living

cottage

couch potato

coup

court

credit card

credit crunch

crops

culprit

currency

current affairs

curriculum

cutting-edge

CV (curriculum vitae)

'cyber-'

D

debit card

defendant

degree

dehydrated

dementia

democracy

demolish

demonstrate

depopulation

deposit

derelict

destination

detached house

detour

develop

diagnosis

die out

discrimination

disembark

dissertation/thesis

dissident

distance learning

divorce

documentary

drought

drug abuse

E

economic growth

ecosystem

ecotourism

editor

election

embark

emigration

employee

employer

endangered

engagement

episode

equestrian

escape from something/someone

estuary/mouth

ethnic cleansing

ethnic minority

euthanasia

exchange rate

excursion

exhaust fumes

exhibition

expenditure

experiment

export

extended family

extinct

extremism

eye-catching

eyesore

F

facilities

faculty (BE)

fast food

fat

fatal
fee
ferry
fertilizer
festival
fiction
first aid
flexitime
food poisoning
fossil fuels
fracking
franchise
free press
futuristic

G

gadget
gated community
geek/nerd
genes
genetically modified foods
genocide
geriatric
germ
get away with something
glacier
global warming
go on strike
gorge
graduate
green
greenhouse effect
guardian
gymnastics

H

hand in your notice
hand luggage
have a picnic

headline
hemisphere
high-rise
high-tech
hilly
homelessness
horoscope
housing estate
human rights
hype
hypochondriac
hypothesis/theory
iceberg

I

ideology
illegal alien
illiterate
immigrate
immigration
immune system
import
income tax
inflation
information technology (IT)
infrastructure
inner city
innocent
innovation
insulation
interest
intern
invest
irrigation
itinerary

J

Jacuzzi
jet lag

jingle

journal

journalism

journey

judge

jury

juvenile

L

labour-saving

latitude

lawyer

lecture

left-wing

let off steam

lifestyle

literacy

live (event)

logo

long-haul

longitude

low-rise

luxury accommodation

M

made redundant (BE)

make progress

malignant

malnourished

manufacturing

marathon

marine life

marketing

martial arts

Master's degree

masterpiece

maternal

maternity leave

matinee

megacity
metropolitan
microchip
minerals
ministry
modernist
monarchy
mortgage
mound
mountain range
multinational corporation
musical

N

nanotechnology
nationalism
nonconformist
non-fiction
nuclear family
nutrients

O

obesity
obsolete
occupation
office block
offspring
on credit
opera
orchestra
organic
outcast
outdated
outskirts
outsource
overcrowding
overdraft
overtime
overweight
ozone layer

P

paparazzi
paragliding
paralysed
paternal
patio
patriotic
pay-per-view
peak/summit
pedestrian precinct
peninsula
pension
performance
personal ads
PhD
pianist
plug
poetry
policy
political asylum
political party
portion
portrait
postgraduate
prescription
presenter
president
priceless
primary education
prime minister
product launch
product placement
profession
proprietor
prosperity
protein
public transport
publisher
pupil

Q

qualifications

R

racism
radical
radiotherapy
rebate
recession
recreational
recycle
referee
referendum
refugee
relatives
renewable energy
reporter
research
reservoir
resign/quit
right-wing
riot
rugged
running track
rural

S

sacked/fired
salary
satellite
scholarship
scuba diving
search engine
secondary education
sedentary
seminar (BE)
senior citizen

sentence

sewage

sexual harassment

shopping mall

short-haul

siblings

side-effects

single-parent family

skyscraper

slogan

slum

smog

snack

soap opera

social life

socialist

solicitor (BE)

special offer

spectators

sponsorship

squad

squatter

stadium

standard of living

standing ovation

state-of-the-art

state school

stepmother and stepfather

still life

stock market

stocks and shares

storey (BE) / story (AE)

structure

subliminal advertising

subscription

suburbs

superpower

surgeon

syllabus

symptom

T

tabloid
take a stroll
target audience
tariff
taxation
technophobe
telesales
tenpin bowling
terminal (n.)
terminology
terrace
terrorism
tertiary education
the elderly
the press
the rush hour
threat (n.)
totalitarian
trade barrier
traffic congestion
trainee
transplant (v.)
trekking
trial (n.)
trip (n)
tutorial (BE)

U

undergraduate
unemployed (adj.)
unemployment benefit
unique selling point (USP)
upbringing
urban
urban sprawl

V

vegetarian
venue
verdict
victim
virus
vitamins
vote

W

wage
weapon
well off
well-designed
well-informed
widow/widower
work-life balance
worthless
wound (n.)

About the Cover Designer

As a young girl growing up in northern Indiana, Sandy MacGowan was greatly influenced by her late father, a professional photographer. That influence, coupled with her love of art, would resurface years later after she received her Bachelor of Arts degree in Fine Arts from Indiana University. Sandy spent most of the next ten years as a computer graphics artist, specialising in speaker-support presentations, medical illustration and graphic design.

While studying 3D computer graphics and animation in Canada, Sandy met her husband, Brian MacGowan. As another computer graphics artist with extensive training in photography, he has provided her with much insight into the quirks and foibles of computer graphics.

While on a career hiatus for motherhood, Sandy once again embraced her early love of photography. Digital photography, along with computer graphics, now enable her to artistically enhance her photos, resulting in the illusion of a painterly effect when viewed either onscreen or as prints.

Sandy currently resides once more in northern Indiana, along with Brian and their two daughters.